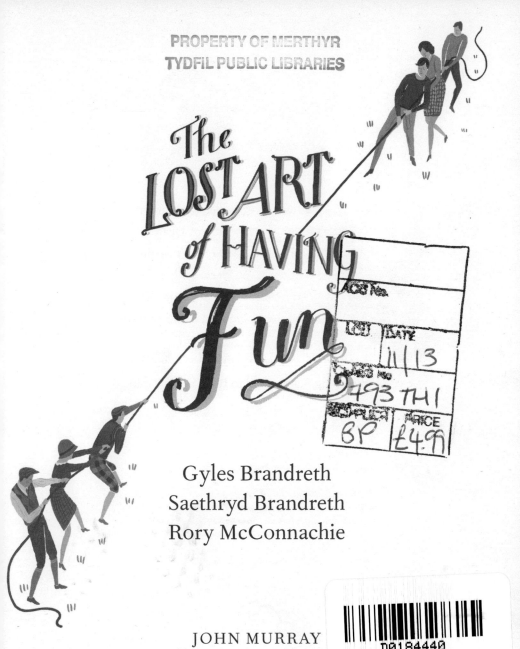

The LOST ART of HAVING Fun

Gyles Brandreth
Saethryd Brandreth
Rory McConnachie

JOHN MURRAY

First published in Great Britain in 2013 by John Murray (Publishers)
An Hachette UK Company

1

© Gyles Brandreth and Saethryd Brandreth 2013

A CIP catalogue record for this title is available from the British Library

Hardback ISBN 978-1-84854-974-6
Ebook ISBN 978-1-84854-975-3

Typeset in Fournier MT by Hewer Text UK Ltd, Edinburgh
Printed and bound by Clays Ltd, St Ives plc

John Murray policy is to use papers that are natural, renewable and
recyclable products and made from wood grown in sustainable forests.
The logging and manufacturing processes are expected to conform
to the environmental regulations of the country of origin.

John Murray (Publishers)
338 Euston Road
London NW1 3BH

www.johnmurray.co.uk

In memory of three generations of grandmothers
who introduced each of us to their favourite games:

Granny Addison (1879–1959)
Granny Brandreth (1914–2009)
Granny Apple (1950–2013)

CONTENTS

3

Analogue Fun in a Digital World 97

Aggression; All Ways; Alphabet Race; Battleships; Boxes; Consequences; Picture Consequences; Crossing Out the Letters; Hangman; Joining Points; Noughts and Crosses; Salvo; Shooting Stars; Sprouts; Word Squares; The Worm; All Square; Columns and Rows; Garden Path; Kayles; Matchboxes; Match-Taker; Maxey; Nim; One-Line Nim; Niminy-Piminy; Odd or Even; Spillikins; Take the Last; Fivestones (Ones; Twos; Threes; Fours; Pecks; Bushels; Claws; Ones Under the Arch; Twos Under the Arch; Threes Under the Arch; Fours Under the Arch; Stables; Toad in the Hole; Snake in the Grass)

4

The Race is On 161

A-Tissue; Balloon Race; Bang Bang Race; Biscuit Race; Blow Ball; Deportment Relay; Doll Dressing; Drop the Lot; Head Space; Knot Race; Map Race; Ankle Race; Back-to-Back Race; Nose Ball; Piggy-Back Race; Three-Legged Race; Newspaper Race; Pick and Cup Race; Potato Race; Spoon Ball; Thimble Race; Tortoise Race; Two-Minute Race

5

Einstein & Friends 189

AA; Acrostics; Alpha; Alphabet Story; Anagrams; Arena; Big Words; Botticelli; Bulls and Cows; Categories; Changelings; Clue Words; Crambo; Crossword; Crosswords; Donkey; Guggenheim; Hidden Words; Leading Lights; Little Words; Proverbs; Rhyme in Time; Scaffold; Short Story; Stairway; Stepping

6
Party Games 251

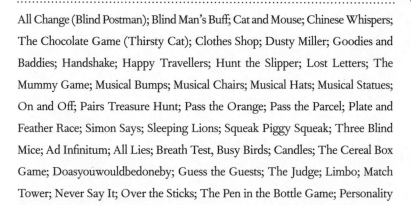

7
Music & Drama 309

8

Country House Weekend 349

9

Seasonal Games 417

Index 459

The LOST ART of HAVING Fun

INTRODUCTIONS

Gyles writes:

Saethryd and Rory and I were born to write this book. Our family has been in the fun and games business for several generations.

My great-grandmother's nephew was George R. Sims (1847–1922), the most prolific and highest-paid journalist of his day. Sims made his name writing for a weekly magazine called *Fun*. Queen Victoria read *Fun* and was amused. Sims also wrote plays and pantomimes, and a sentimental ballad entitled *It is Christmas Day in the Workhouse*, which, on long winter evenings in the good old days, the head of the family would recite by heart, with feeling, at the fireside, between a game of Charades and a chorus of 'My Old Man said "Follow the Van"' around the piano.

My great-great-grandfather was Benjamin Brandreth (1809–1880), who left England for America in 1833 and made a fortune manufacturing 'Brandreth's Pills' – vegetable pills that claimed to cure everything. Herman Melville, the great American novelist, immortalised Brandreth's pills in *Moby Dick*. P. T. Barnum, the circus king, admired Brandreth, above all others, for his extraordinary marketing skills. To help promote his unique medicine, Brandreth published *Brandreth's Puzzle Book*, a compendium of his favourite games and puzzles.

I have a copy of that book, and of a dozen and more books of Victorian family entertainment handed down to me by my father, Charles Brandreth (1910–1981). My father was a master of the lost art of having fun. He had a repertoire of parlour recitations he could call on; he was a dab-hand at close-up parlour magic; he was an expert on the rules of all the best parlour games.

Indeed, it is through a game – the world's best-selling board game – that my father met my mother and that I and Saethryd and Rory are here to tell the tale. In 1936 the American games company Parker Brothers began licensing Monopoly for sale outside of the United States. The first British games of Monopoly went on sale that Christmas. My father, aged twenty-six, bought one of them (at Selfridges department store in London's Oxford Street) and, looking for someone to play the game with, found himself introduced to my mother, Alice Addison, then aged twenty-two. Twenty weeks later, Charles and Alice ran off together and were married. Thirty-four years later, as the official European Monopoly Champion, I came third in the World Monopoly Championships in New York. I have always done my best to do the family proud.

As a boy, while I was a Monopoly mini-master, a bit of a devil at dominoes, and quite clued-up on Cluedo, Scrabble was really my board game of choice. I went to a boarding school called Bedales where I played Scrabble on Wednesday afternoons with the school's founder, John Badley (1865–1967). Mr Badley, who had been a friend of Oscar Wilde, among others, was a skilful Scrabble player and, though in his late nineties when I was playing against him, invariably won our matches. I accused him of using words that were obsolete. He assured me that they had been current when he first learnt them.

I founded the National Scrabble Championships in 1971, and am now President of the Association of British Scrabble Players. For some years

I was also a director of Spears Games, manufacturers of Scrabble and assorted other great indoor games – two of which, I am proud to say, I invented. (Rory is especially keen on my Alice in Wonderland game.) My mother was also a games inventor and anyone who has played her word game, Haathi (manufactured for a while by my sister, Hester, in South Africa) will know that it is the most challenging – and satisfying – word game of them all.

I hope you are getting the idea. We Brandreths are into games. And the games we are most into are the games you will find here in the pages that follow. These aren't board games or card games or games requiring special equipment. These are simply our family's all-time favourites and most of them are, unashamedly, *old* favourites.

The oldest of all is probably Blind Man's Buff. You know how it goes? A blindfolded player rushes about the room trying to catch hold of the other sighted players, who dodge out of his way. When the blindfolded player catches his victim, he has to guess who it is, and, if he is right, to change places with him. In its origins the game is connected with the early rites of human sacrifice and dates back to the time of the one-eyed god Odin, chief deity of Norse mythology. Through the centuries it has been known as Billie Blind, Hoodle-cum-Blind and Blind Harrie, but it's a great game despite its gruesome heritage. Rory (born in 2006) has a particular soft spot for it.

One of Rory's grandfathers (me) has a special fondness for Charades, another of the oldest games in the book. The name comes from the Spanish *charrada*, meaning the chatter of clowns. The game came to Britain from the Continent in 1776, but it didn't come into its own until the mid to late nineteenth century, during the Victorian heyday of home entertainment when no house party was complete without a session of Charades or Sardines – or Apple Ducking, a particular royal favourite. In the 1980s I used to appear in a TV version of Charades called *Give Us A Clue*. It was a fun show to watch, as I remember, but it was an even more fun game to play.

That's the point, really. *Doing* is more fun than *watching*. And our hope is that this book will guide you and your family and friends as you play these games together and rediscover the lost art of having fun.

Play is important. You don't need to take my word for it. Friedrich Schiller, the great German poet and philosopher, took time off from writing *William Tell* to remind us that 'man only plays when in the full meaning of the word he is a man, and he is only completely a man when he plays'. Johan Huizinga, the Dutch historian and author of *Homo Ludens*, the definitive study of the place of play in our culture, put it like this:

> *Play adorns life, amplifies it and is to that extent a necessity, both for the individual – as a life function – and for society by reason of the meaning it contains, its significance, its expressive value, its spiritual and cultural associations, in short, as a cultural function. The expression of it satisfies all kinds of cultural needs.*

So there you go. It turns out this book is more significant than any of us realised. Have fun with *The Lost Art of Having Fun* and do yourself – and society – a favour.

Saethryd writes:

Right, well, before Dad lays claim to be the Dalai Lama of dominoes or whatever, I think we should probably get a few things straight.

Games are making a comeback; and that's a cultural zeitgeist I think even my never-exactly-shy-and-retiring father would probably be hesitant to take credit for. We are not the only family in Britain who are rediscovering our love of a good game. Driven by the recession, and our overwhelmingly materialistic popular culture, the good folk of these fair isles are fighting back. The popularity of shows like *The Great British Bake Off* and *Kirsty's Homemade Home* demonstrate that we are returning to the make-do-and-mend ethos that made Britain great in the first place. There's been a shift away from buying mass-produced to making our own . . . and that includes making our own fun.

Also, is it just me or are there suddenly children *everywhere*? It's a veritable explosion: you can't escape the little blighters – toddlers running around cafés, babies bawling on buses, pubs doubling up as daycare. I was at a friend's house the other day and an eight-month-old just *emerged* from under their sofa – gave me quite a shock, I can tell you. And it's not just us regular folk that are at it. There were at least three of them in Downing Street last time I checked and a brand new one at Kensington Palace.

Now, just as we Brandreths don't lay claim to being the progenitors of the Great Games Revolution, neither do we claim to be responsible for the baby boom – though my parents do have six grandchildren and counting, so we are not doing too badly. But what all this means is that there is a whole new generation of parents who are rediscovering the joy of games. The era of all-night parties and responsibility-free Sundays may be long gone, but that doesn't mean we want to stop having fun, far from it. It's just that now we are less likely to go out, especially with the cost of the babysitter and the state of the economy, and more likely to have our friends round in the evening for a bottle of wine, a couple of rounds of the Hat Game (page 361) and a late-night Limbo (page 297) before waking up in the morning and playing Sardines (page 376) with the kids. (A nice cosy hiding-spot where you can lie down is recommended if you've had a little too much fun late-night limboing.)

One of my favourite chapters in the book is *Analogue Fun in a Digital World*. I, too, am very much guilty of the 'Here's an iPhone now let me talk to my friends for thirty minutes in peace' school of parenting. And not just out of the house. I'll share a little, and some may say inconsequential, story with you; one which will never win me the Parent of the Year award but is genuinely the moment I rediscovered the joys of games for every occasion.

Rory is an only child and, if we are being honest here, which I hope we are, I can be a somewhat lazy parent. The thing no one really says out loud about kids, especially young kids, is they can be – *whisper it* – quite boring. There, I said it. Sometimes the incessant chatter and non-stop demands can be dull, dull, dull, so when it came to mealtimes I had a tendency to just bung Rory, and his fish fingers, down in front of the telly, so that I could get on with the important business of being me, in other words, doing the laundry, checking Facebook and reading *Heat* magazine.

I started to feel guilty. I've read the books. I know family mealtime is important, so I made a conscious decision to rectify this. Even if it was just going to be me and Rory, and he was the only one eating, we were going to sit down at the table together and have some quality time, gosh darn it.

The first day, there we are: him sat there pushing his peas around his plate; me with my packet of peanuts and half a glass of corner-shop cava to add to the sense of occasion. By the third time I'd asked him how school was that day, my cava disappearing a *little* more quickly than it really ought to have, Rory's staring at the TV like it's a long-lost lover about to be deported back to Mexico.

Then it happened. I, being a master of dinner party conversation, asked (again), 'How's the fish?'; to which he replied 'Chips'; then I said 'Peas'; then he said 'Potatoes'; I said' Mash'; he said 'Monster'; I said 'Truck'; and, all of a sudden, we were playing this quite surreal but actually really enjoyable word association game. All of a sudden we were having fun! Okay, we are easily entertained, but it was that moment, that shift from two people being there but not really being present, to two people genuinely being absorbed in what was going on and really enjoying each other's company that was important.

So that's what this book is all about: having fun with your family and friends. That's why there are no solo games included. (Perhaps *Fun for One* should be our next book?) It was also important to us that the games be accessible, which is why we haven't included games that need specialised equipment, such as cards or board games. (We'll move on to card games and board games when we have sorted the solo games.)

This book does not claim to be a definitive work. It is simply a collection of our favourite games, all tried and tested, with enough of a range included to enable you to find the right game for the occasion, age and temperament.

Each family has its own traditions (I'm yet to meet another family who enjoy a game of Denk-Fix on Christmas Day) and we would love to hear yours. So, in the spirit of mixing old with new, the analogue with the digital, we'd love it if you would visit the *Lost Art of Having Fun* Facebook page or Twitter and let us know all about the games you play in *your* family. It is the perfect place to upload photos of a round of 'Are you there, Moriarty?' (page 15), share your car journey classics and wrangle over the correct rules for Charades (page 318). We've got some classic footage of my granny playing Bun Biting (page 408) which may yet see the light of day . . .

Of course, no one is saying you have to be some sort of all-singing, all-dancing, all-games-playing super-family. Sometimes there is nothing better than shoving an iPhone in the kids' direction or turning on the telly for a couple of hours' peace. Playing these games, we all really enjoy ourselves and each other's company. And, because I know I've had that time when I've been really present and genuinely enjoyed myself, and my child, and our time together, I don't feel guilty genuinely enjoying taking some time out of motherhood to play the Post-It Note Game (page 373) with my friends, or going out to dinner or work, or reading a trashy book or whatever takes my fancy. It's all about balance, living in the moment, being present, forgetting your worries and remembering that, for all its trials and tribulations, life is meant to be *fun*.

Actually, maybe Dad's whole Dalai Lama of the dominoes schtick wasn't so off after all . . .

Rory writes:

Ah, Dalai what? Er, Dalai who? Yes, it is true, I do like playing the games with Mum. And with Granddad. I've not really written a lot of this book. Mum keeps telling me I have, but I'm pretty sure she's lying. What I have done is played lots of the games and let you know the ones I really like.

Plus I've made a couple of really awesome jokes.

Rainy Day GAMES

Here are some games *to play on a
wet Wednesday in the school holidays.
They are also ideal for when the family is
gathered together on a Sunday afternoon
after a mouth-watering medley of all things
roasted ('Extra bread sauce over here,
please; thank you very much'). The fire is
burning brightly, Granny is dozing in the
corner, and it would be criminal to turn on
the television when you could be having
some good old-fashioned fun instead. So,
without further ado, let the games begin!*

'Are you there, Moriarty?'

This game has been a rainy day favourite for more than a hundred years, since the heyday, in fact, of the great detective Sherlock Holmes and his arch-enemy, the elusive Professor James Moriarty, the 'Napoleon of Crime'.

It is a game for two players and an audience; and everybody can take a turn, if they dare!

Once you have your players and your audience, all you need are two blindfolds and two rolled-up newspapers . . . The scene is set for a duel to the death (well, almost).

The two players are blindfolded and made to lie flat on the floor, face down, each grasping the other's left wrist with his left hand. In their right hands they hold their weapons: the rolled-up newspapers.

On the command 'Go!' the first player calls out 'Are you there, Moriarty?' to which the other player must reply 'Yes'. As he does so, the first player will attempt to wallop him with a single well-aimed blow from his rolled-up newspaper, judging the second player's location by where his voice is coming from. To avoid the attack, of course, an artful player will cry 'Yes' in one place and quickly roll to another (without letting go of his opponent's left wrist).

Players take it in turns to do the asking and walloping and the replying and rolling. The player with the greater number of direct hits after a set time is the winner.

The Balloon Bashing Game

For this game you will need a blown-up balloon, a rolled-up newspaper, a blindfold and at least four players.

The players stand in a circle and, one at a time, take it in turns to put on the blindfold and stand in the middle. The blindfold player is given the rolled-up newspaper to hold and the blown-up balloon is placed on the ground somewhere inside the circle. The blindfold player is then twirled around three times and told 'Bash the balloon!' He can then have three goes at bashing the balloon. If he manages to hit it the first time, he scores 3 points. If he hits it the second time, he scores 2 points. If he tries three times to bash it but misses every time, he scores nothing.

After each player has had two chances to be the blindfold balloon basher in the centre of the circle, the player with the highest number of points is declared the winner and gets given the balloon as a prize.

Catch the Keys

For this game you need a large clear room, a large jangly key ring and at least four players.

Blindfold two of the players and get them to stand facing each other about three metres apart. Now somewhere in between them throw down the key ring. As soon as the players hear the key ring clatter to the ground they can move towards it and try to pick it up. The first player to find the key ring wins a point. The players take it in turns to be blindfolded and to try and catch the keys. After a set number of rounds the player with the highest score is the winner.

The Crocodile Game

This game is named after the famous crocodile in J. M. Barrie's wonderful story and play, *Peter Pan*. The story of the crocodile goes something like this. Once upon a time, the crocodile, who lived in Neverland, ate the hand of Peter Pan's arch-enemy, Captain Hook. He found the hand so tasty he was eager to eat the rest of the rascally pirate and pursued the Captain everywhere. However, Captain Hook could always tell when the crocodile was coming because the animal had also swallowed an alarm clock. And it was a clock with a very loud tick. Whenever the crocodile got near, the Captain was forewarned by the sound, which is how he managed to survive for so long. He survived, in fact, until the day the clock stopped.

When you play the Crocodile Game you must make sure the clock you use is well wound up, has an audible tick, and doesn't stop.

Begin by sending one of the players out of the room and, while the player is outside, let everyone else decide on somewhere clever to hide the clock: behind the curtains, under a cushion, behind some books, in the piano stool, under the sofa, anywhere, in fact, so long as the clock's tick can still be heard.

When the clock is well hidden, the player who has been outside returns and has to find it. He will be led, of course, by the ticking. When he finds the clock, another player leaves the room, the clock is hidden again, and the second player then returns to find it. Time each player who looks for the clock and the player who manages the task in the shortest time is declared the winner.

Dead-Pan

This game is all about getting the giggles; or rather, it's about trying desperately *not* to get the giggles.

The players sit or stand in a circle, and one of them is chosen to be the leader.

The leader nudges the player on his left, who nudges the player on *his* left, who nudges the player on *her* left, and so on round the circle back to the leader.

The leader now tweaks the ear of the player on his left, who tweaks the ear of the player on *his* left, and so on round the circle once more.

For the third and subsequent rounds the leader shakes his neighbour's hand, or tickles him under the chin, or blows in his ear, or pulls his nose, or does whatever amuses him, and the other players do the same round the circle.

The idea is that the players should perform all these actions without showing any sign of amusement. Anyone who smiles, let alone sniggers, smirks, giggles, has hysterics or cannot contain even the tiniest of tiny chuckles is immediately disqualified and leaves the circle.

Whoever laughs last, laughs most, as they are declared the winner.

Do This! Do That!

This game is a variation of the classic children's game Simon Says (page 281), and will be enjoyed by the young and the young-at-heart alike.

One player is chosen as the leader and she stands out in front of all the other players who must face her. She will then call out 'Do this!' or 'Do that!' and perform an action at the same time. When the leader says 'Do this!', the players *must* do whatever she is doing; and when she says 'Do that!' they *must not*.

So when the leader says 'Do this!' and claps her hands, the players must all clap their hands; when she says this 'Do this!' and scratches her ear, the players must all scratch their ears. But when she says 'Do that!' and puts her hands on her hips, nobody must move. Anyone caught obeying an order on the command 'Do that!' drops out. Anyone who does not move quickly enough on the command 'Do this!' retires as well.

The last player in is the winner.

Fanning the Kipper

A fun and silly racing game which is not as easy to play as it sounds and which brings out the competitive spirit in even the most mild-mannered of souls.

In our family the game is played every Christmas Eve and the winner is awarded the much coveted Kipper Trophy, which takes pride of place on the recipient's mantelpiece until the following year.

The game works like this. Each player is given a 'kipper' – a piece of flimsy tissue paper, about twenty centimetres long and ten centimetres wide, cut in the shape of a fish – and a folded newspaper to use as a 'fan'.

The 'kippers' are lined up at the starting-point of the course, with each player standing behind his fish, fan at the ready. In our family, we race along the hallway, but you can race from one side of the sitting room to the other or around the kitchen.

'On your marks, get set, go!' Players have to fan their kippers along the course by waving their newspapers just behind the kipper's tail. The first player whose kipper crosses the finishing line is the winner.

Anyone caught touching their kipper will be disqualified *immediately*. You have been warned!

Rory says: I love this game.

Going Through the Motions

The players form a circle. The first player performs any action he chooses – tapping his foot, twitching his nose, winking one eye, closing the other, bobbing up and down, or whatever.

The second player must copy the action of the first player and at the same time perform an additional action of her choice.

The third player must copy the actions of both the first and second player and then add an extra action of his own. And so the game progresses on round the circle, with each player copying all the actions of the previous players and adding an extra action.

Any player who fails to add an action, or misses out an action, or falls over in a state of confusion and exhaustion, is out of the game. The last player left tapping, twitching, winking, nodding, bobbing, hopping and waving, is the winner.

Grab the Bell

To play this invigorating rainy day game you will need one Leader, one Victim, at least four other players, a blindfold and a small hand-bell.

Gyles says: Victorians, of course, kept small hand-bells in their parlours: they used them to summon the servants. These days they are in short supply in many modern houses. You could always replace the hand-bell with another object that could be noisy if picked up wrongly – a football rattle, a jar of beads, you get the idea.

The players sit on the floor in a circle with the blindfolded Victim sitting in the centre. The Leader stands outside the circle. The hand-bell is placed on the ground just in front of the blindfold Victim.

When everyone is in position, the Leader will point silently to one of the seated players, who must get up and creep as quietly as possible towards the Victim and try to grab the bell. If the Victim hears a noise, he will point to the direction from which he thinks the player is coming. If he's right, the Leader will say 'Well done, you've caught him', and the player who was creeping towards the bell has to return to her place. The Leader will then point to another player, who will also try to creep silently towards the Victim and grab the bell without being caught. If the Victim points in the wrong direction, the Leader says nothing and the creeping player can carry on creeping. As soon as a player manages to grab the bell, the round is over and the Victim takes off his blindfold, joins the circle and the clever player who got the bell becomes the new Victim.

Rory says: I love this game.

Horseshoe

For this parlour game, you don't need horses and you don't even need horseshoes. All you need are four ordinary upright chairs and *sixteen* old shoes.

Position the four chairs in a small circle, blindfold the four players and get each of them to sit on one of the chairs. Now put the sixteen shoes on the floor somewhere in the middle of the circle. On the command 'Go!' the players must get off their chairs and scramble on the floor for a shoe. Once they have found a shoe, they must return to their own chairs and place it under one of the four legs. They must then go back and find a second shoe, return to their chair with that, put it under the second chair-leg, go back for a third shoe, and finally, of course, for a fourth.

The first player to have placed four shoes on the four legs of his or her chair and then be again seated on the chair is the winner.

Hunt the Ring

How long is a piece of string? Well, for this game it needs to be as long as necessary to form a loop of string that can be held by all the players standing in a circle. To play the game, you will need the right length of string, a simple finger-ring and a minimum of six players.

Begin by threading your long piece of string through the ring and tying the ends of the string together to form one large loop. Arrange the players in a circle and give them the string to hold, but first put one player in the centre of the circle. On the command 'Go!' the players in the circle must run the string through their hands, which means that the ring will be constantly on the move. The 'man in the middle' has the unenviable task of finding the moving ring. To do this he has three chances to touch one of the player's hands. When he touches a hand, it must be opened and if the ring is underneath then the man in the middle is victorious and changes place with the player who was hiding the ring. If the man in the middle fails to find the ring after three attempts, he drops out of the game.

No one wins this game, but if the string and the ring are circulated at speed a lot of fun can be had by all.

Hunt the Thimble

A classic Victorian parlour game if ever there was one, Hunt the Thimble is played less often today – if only because there seem to be fewer thimbles about than once there were. Not to worry; any small object will work just as well. It can be anything you like, but it shouldn't be smaller than a sugar lump or larger than an egg cup. You will need at least three people to play this game, but the more the merrier.

A room is selected, and a player is chosen to 'hide' the thimble while the other players are outside. The thimble should be placed in a spot where it is completely visible but not immediately noticeable.

The players then come back into the room and begin to hunt for the thimble.

Each player, as soon as she spots the thimble, must sit down without saying a word and without drawing attention to the thimble's location. The last player to spot the thimble – and you'll marvel at how long it takes some people to notice something that's staring them in the face – is the loser. It is their turn to hide the thimble next . . . but it adds to the fun if they have to perform a forfeit first.

Kaleidoscope

All the players but one stand in a line facing the remaining player. In turn they tell her what 'colour' they are. If there are three players, they might be red, white and blue. If there are six, they might be black, blue, red, pink, yellow and turquoise. All the colours of the rainbow, and every colour besides, are allowed, but each player must choose a different colour.

Once all the players in the line-up have declared their colour, the remaining player, who is facing them, has to close her eyes. While her eyes are shut the players in the line-up all switch positions, and when the player facing them reopens her eyes, she has to identify their colours.

Sounds simple? Try it and see.

Kim's Game

This game takes its name from Rudyard Kipling's much-loved novel, *Kim*. The story's eponymous hero, an orphan growing up in India at the end of the nineteenth century, plays the game as part of his training to become a spy. The game, a true classic, is essentially a test of memory and observation. It requires two or more players and a bit of preparation.

The preparation. Prior to the game, gather up twenty or more different objects and place them on a tray or a table. The objects can be anything that is small and recognisable – an apple, an orange, a cup, a saucer, a thimble, a sugar lump, a ten-pound note, a pen, a pencil sharpener, an egg cup, a bar of chocolate, a playing card, a xylophone hammer, a potato, a copy of this book – anything will do. The items are placed at random and then the whole assemblage is covered with a cloth.

The play. When the preparation is complete, everybody gathers round and the cloth is removed. The players have just thirty seconds to study the collection of objects in front of them before the cloth is replaced. Each player is then given a pencil and some paper with which to list all the objects that they can remember.

A player scores 1 point for each object remembered, but loses a point if he or she lists any object that was not there.

The player scoring the highest number of points is the winner.

Gyles says: I love this game and played it first when I was in the Cub Scouts almost sixty years ago. The game was a particular favourite of Robert Baden-Powell, Rudyard Kipling's friend and the founder of the Boy Scouts and Girl Guides movements. Baden-Powell based a lot of his ideas on Kipling's writings and had a good philosophy of life. On 4 July 1911, in a letter to a friend, he wrote: 'I know my weak points and am only thankful that I have managed to get along in spite of them! I think that's the policy for this world: be glad of what you have got, and not miserable about what you would like to have had, and not over-anxious about what the future will bring.'

Newspaper Fancy Dress

Each player is given a newspaper and some sticky tape, from which to make a fancy-dress costume. The players have ten minutes in which to do this. When the ten minutes have elapsed, the players parade around the room, and the winner is the player who is judged to have made the cleverest, most amusing, or most original costume.

Nose to Nose

This is a game for close friends and those with sturdy immune systems.

The players divide into teams and each team stands in a straight line. Each team leader is given a matchbox cover and on the command 'Get set!' they fix this on to the end of their nose. On the word 'Go!' they turn and do their best to transfer the matchbox to the nose of whoever happens to be next in line. The game is a race, and the first team to have got its matchbox from the first nose to the last wins.

No hands are allowed, and when a matchbox falls to the floor the team has to start all over again.

One-Minute Walk

For this game you will need a watch with a second hand, two or more players and an umpire.

The umpire begins by covering up any visible clocks in the place of play and by confiscating all the players' watches. He then lines up the players at one side of the room and tells them they have exactly sixty seconds in which to travel from one side of the room to the opposite side. They can travel at any speed they like, but they mustn't stop moving *even for a moment*. Players who do stop moving, or who reach the opposite side before the minute is up, are out. The player who is nearest the opposite side at the very second the minute is up wins the game.

This game sounds like a somewhat silly and simple exercise. In fact it is an exciting game, the mastery of which calls for an uncanny sense of timing. When you are crossing a small room, a minute takes very much longer to pass than you might imagine.

Picasso

Pablo Picasso once said: 'Painting is a blind man's profession. He paints not what he sees, but what he feels.' In this game the words of the Master are taken somewhat literally. To play it you will need some simple equipment and an even number of players.

The players are divided into pairs and each couple sit back to back. One of the pair is given a piece of paper, a pencil and something to act as a drawing board; the other is given an object such as a pineapple, an egg whisk, a chess piece or a rubber duck. It can be anything, so long as it is interesting. Without telling their partner what the object is, nor what it is used for, the player must describe it: its size, shape, how it feels, etc. The partner has to draw the object on the basis of the description given, following the directions as best they can.

At the end of the game, either the most accurate or the most remarkable illustration wins the prize. Almost certainly, you will end up with more than a few Surrealist works of art, but don't worry. As Picasso also pointed out, 'Art is noble play.'

Pippety-Pop, Poppety-Pip

All but one of the players sits in a circle, with the extra player standing in the centre. The man in the middle then revolves at speed pointing at different players and calling out 'Pippety-pop' or 'Poppety-pip'. Whenever he calls out 'Pippety-pop', the player at whom he is pointing must reply 'Pip', and whenever it's 'Poppety-pip' the answer must be 'Pop'. Any player who hesitates or says 'Pip' when it should be 'Pop' or 'Pop' when it should be 'Pip' drops out.

The last player left in the circle is the winner and becomes the man in the middle for the next round.

Shopping List

This game is good for a large number of players.

One of the players is the shopper. The other players, in teams of four to six, represent rival department stores. The shopper calls out items from his shopping list, which may be prepared beforehand or may be made up on the spur of the moment. The items on the list should be objects which some, at least, of the players might reasonably be expected to have about their persons: an iPhone, a safety pin, a bus ticket, a key ring with at least four keys on, a lip gloss, a pair of socks.

A point is awarded to the first 'store' (team) to supply the shopper with each item, and the store with the most points at the end of the game is the winner.

Sitting and Standing

Here's another parlour game that calls for one Leader, one Victim, at least four other players and a blindfold.

The players all stand in a straight line facing the Victim (who wears a thick blindfold) and the Leader (who doesn't). When everyone is in position, the Leader will give the players the 'thumbs down' sign, which means that they must all sit down. A moment later she will give the 'thumbs up' sign, which means they must all stand up. Then she repeats the 'thumbs down' sign, then 'thumbs up', then 'thumbs down', 'thumbs up', 'thumbs down', 'thumbs up', 'thumbs down', and so on. Each time the players stand up or sit down, they must do so as silently as they possibly can. No pushing and shoving, no stumbling and shuffling and certainly no giggling!

After the Leader has given several 'thumbs up' and several 'thumbs down' signs, she will say to the Victim, 'Are they standing or sitting now?' If the Victim gives the correct answer, he has won the round, takes off his blindfold and another player becomes the Victim. However, if he gets if wrong, he has lost the round and stays on as Victim while the leader gives a few more 'thumbs up' and 'thumbs down' signs before asking the Victim once again 'Are they standing or sitting now?'

The game goes on until all the players have had a chance to be the Victim or until it's teatime – whichever is the sooner.

'This is my nose . . .'

Everyone sits in a circle and the first player begins by touching a part of his body while at the same time saying that it is another part of his body and adding the name of one of the other players. The named player must then touch some part of her body, saying it is another part and mentioning a third player. And so it goes on until a player hesitates or says he is touching a certain part of his body when he really is.

The game could begin like this:

PLAYER ONE (touching heel): This is my nose, Charles.

CHARLES (touching calf): This is my ankle, Alice.

ALICE (touching eye): This is my chin, Jennifer.

JENNIFER (touching elbow): This is my mouth, Virginia.

VIRGINIA (touching hip): This is my ear, Ben.

BEN (touching knee): This is my head, Hester.

HESTER (touching cheek): This is my neck, Charles.

CHARLES (touching hair): This is my hair . . .

Whoops! Charles has slipped up and must drop out of the game. The last player left in the circle is the winner. And, of course, the faster it is played, the more fun it is.

'Up Jenkins!'

This old rainy day favourite is a light-hearted game of observation and deduction which offers plenty of scope for bluffing and general merriment. It works best when played at speed.

You will need an even number of players, a coin (or a ring or pebble or other small object) and a table for the players to sit at.

The players are divided into two equal teams and are seated on opposite sides of a table. If the table is small and the players are squashed together this only adds to the fun. The members of one team pass the coin from hand to hand below the table. When the leader of the opposing team calls 'Up Jenkins!', the players on the team with the coin raise their hands, with fists clenched, well above the table. One fist, of course, will be concealing the coin. The leader of the opposing team then calls 'Down Jenkins!', and the raised hands must be slapped down on the table with palms flat.

The opposing team now has to guess which hand the coin is under.

The leader confers with his team-mates and then taps the hand that he thinks conceals the coin. That hand is raised, and if the coin is revealed then the guessing team scores a point; otherwise the team with the coin scores a point.

The team then changes roles for the next round. The winners are the team with the most points when an agreed number of rounds have been played.

If there are quite a few of you, the game may also be played so that the guessing team is allowed three guesses to discover the hand concealing the coin. Three points are scored if the first guess is correct, 2 points if the second guess is correct, and 1 point if the third guess is correct.

Saethryd says: If you find you have a natural talent for 'Up Jenkins!', you might be interested to know that the Welsh still hold a world championship of their version – Tippit – each year. Head to the Red Lion pub in the village of Llanafan Fwar in Powys if you fancy your chances . . .

Why? When? How? Where?

One player is sent from the room, while the others agree on an object or an individual for him to have to identify on his return. The object can be anything – from a lemon to the Eiffel Tower – and the person can be anyone in fact or fiction, so long as they are someone that everybody playing the game is likely to have heard of.

When the player returns, he must ask each person in turn the question, 'Why do you like it?'

The other players must answer the question sensibly, but without divulging the actual identity of the chosen object or person. For example, suppose the person chosen is Victoria Beckham; the answers to the first question could range from 'I love fashion' to 'I like things that are spicy'.

The questioner then asks everyone in turn, 'When do you like it?', to which he could receive answers as varied as 'At the London Olympics opening ceremony' or 'When I'm getting dressed in the morning'.

Then he asks 'How do you like it?' and 'Where do you like it?', and no doubt receives all sorts of interesting and sometimes, quite frankly, bizarre answers.

When he has put his four questions to the company and has considered the answers, he is allowed three guesses. If he identifies the mystery object or person with one of his guesses, he wins the round.

Players take it in turn to leave the room and the game can continue for as many rounds as you fancy . . . or until the rain has stopped.

CAR Journey GAMES

Gyles says: As a wise man once decreed, it is not the destination but the journey that matters; which is why in this section you will find a plethora of word games, observation games, and story-telling delights. 'Are we nearly there yet?' You'll hope not.

Rory says: If there's one thing I hate it's being bored. And if there's one time when I'm more likely to be bored than any other it's when I'm in the car, cooped up with nothing to do for hour and hours and hours on end, which is why Mum (and I) love to play games — though what I really want is for her to buy one of those super-cool, fancy, awesome cars which have DVD players built into the back of the seats, then I can watch TV all the time.

Saethryd says: That's not happening.

Rory says: But James' mum has one.

Saethryd says: It's still not happening.

Rory says: That's not fair.

Gyles says: 'I Spy' anyone?

ALPHABET GAMES

• • •

First off, let's get the engine revving with some alphabet games. These are spoken word games based around the alphabet that are perfect to play with children (and grown-ups) of any age. The wonderful thing about them is that they are very adaptable so can be as simple or as challenging as you wish.

'A was an Aardvark …'

This is one of those alphabet games where players take it in turns to think of a suitable word beginning with the right letter of the alphabet and when they fail to do so they drop out. As it is one of the simpler alphabet games, it is a good one to play with the kids.

The first player has to think of something beginning with A – an apple or an antelope or an army or an ape – and the other players have to tell the story of that something right the way through from B to W (nobody bothers with X, Y and Z). When they get to W, they have to start again at B and go on until only one player is left telling the story. That player is the winner.

Here's an example. It's a gripping and poignant saga about an aardvark, a little animal that's a cross between an anteater and an armadillo, and, by the sounds of it, he didn't have a very good day.

A was an aardvark;
B bought it;
C caught it;
D drowned it;
E entertained it;
F fried it;
G guzzled it;
H hid it;

I ignored it;

J joked about it;

K kissed it;

L loved it;

M mothered it;

N needed it;

O ogled it;

P peeped at it;

Q questioned it;

R raced with it;

S sat on it;

T took it;

U upset it;

V valued it;

W wasted it.

And now we start a second round with the letter B. 'B was a banana . . .'

Initial answers

One of the players is chosen to be the questioner for the first round. He asks any appropriate question, which must be answered by each of the other players in turn. Each player's answer must consist of words beginning with their initials.

For example, to the question, 'What kind of food do you like?' Brad Pitt might reply 'Baked potatoes', Angelina Jolie might reply 'Apricot jam', and Zahara Jolie-Pitt might decide that she did not want to play such a silly game! Or Gyles might say 'Granary bread', Saethryd 'Salty bacon' and Rory 'Raspberry macaroons' (if he was feeling particularly precocious).

The aim of the game is to come up with an answer that makes some sort of sense. A player who fails to give a satisfactory answer within five seconds drops out. The last player left answering questions is the winner and gets to be the questioner for the next round.

Last and First

Acategory is chosen – Birds, Towns, Rivers, TV programmes, Marxist Historians, or whatever. The first player calls out any word belonging to the chosen category. The second player calls out another, beginning with the last letter of the previous word, and so on.

For example, if the chosen category was Animals, the words called out might be:

Elephant
Tiger
Rat
Toad
Dromedary
Yak . . .

All the words called out must belong to the chosen category and no word may be repeated. If a player fails to think of a word or calls out a word which does not belong to the category or which has already been used, then she drops out of the game. The last player left in is the winner.

The Parson's Cat

The first player launches the game by declaring, 'The parson's cat is an amiable cat and his name is Archibald.' The next player then suggests, 'The parson's cat is an adventurous cat and his name is Andrew.' The third player finds that 'The parson's cat is an amorous cat and his name is Albert.'

And so it goes on around the group until all the players have come up with an adjective and a name beginning with A.

Then they must find adjectives and names beginning with B, then C, and so on until they get to the fact that 'The parson's cat is a zealous cat and his name is Zebediah.'

The letters Q and X can be omitted, but anyone failing to come up with an adjective or a name for any other letter drops out.

Gyles says: A parson is a member of the clergy, and thus I like to play a variation on this game involving all sorts of ecclesiastical figures and other characters whose lives involve a spiritual dimension – again listed alphabetically. Here's how you might start:

'The archbishop's cat is an adventurous cat . . .'
'The bishop's cat is a brave cat . . .'
'The cardinal's cat is a cheerful cat . . .'
'The dean's cat is a delightful cat . . .'

'The evangelist's cat is an evil cat . . .'
'The friar's cat is a fat cat . . .'
'The guru's cat is a great cat . . .'
'The heathen's cat is a healthy cat . . .'
'The imam's cat is an individual cat . . .'
'The Jehovah's Witness's cat is a joyful cat . . .'

Keep going, if you can!

Traveller's Alphabet

Traveller's Alphabet is a slightly more demanding form of alphabet sequence game. Each player in turn asks the player on her left two questions: 'Where are you going?' and 'What will you do when you get there?' The replies consist of the name of a country and the description of an activity using a verb, adjective and noun, all beginning with the same letter. The first player's replies must begin with the letter A, the second B, the third C, and so on.

For example, if Mary, Edward and David are playing together, the conversation might go like this:

MARY: Where are you going?
DAVID: Australia.
MARY: What will you do when you get there?
DAVID: Assist aged Aborigines.
DAVID: Where are you going?
EDWARD: Belgium.
DAVID: What will you do when you get there?
EDWARD: Buy big boots.
EDWARD: Where are you going?
MARY: China.
EDWARD: What will you do when you get there?
MARY: Carve cheap chopsticks.

MARY: Where are you going?

DAVID: Denmark.

MARY: What will you do when you get there?

DAVID: Dig deep dykes.

Any player who fails to reply within a reasonable time limit drops out of the game.

If you are playing with very sophisticated and clever players, you can insist that the answer is relevant to the country named – in which case David would now be out because we associate dykes with Holland, not Denmark, don't we?

The winner is the last player left in.

MIXED TRAVELLING BAG

• • •

Next up, we *have a mixed bag of journey jollies. You'll find word games, number games, and even a game which involves sitting in total silence (which we imagine might prove quite popular with the older members of the group).*

Buzz, Fizz and Buzz-Fizz

Buzz, Fizz and Buzz-Fizz are three closely related games which are all very silly, surprisingly challenging and lots of fun.

All you have to do to play them is count from one to infinity. Sounds simple, but there's a catch. Players call out numbers as they count in turn, player one calling 'One', the second player calling 'Two', the third player 'Three', and so on, round and round, as quickly as possible.

Are you ready?

Here's the catch: if Buzz is being played, then the word 'buzz' must be substituted for every multiple of 5 and substituted for the digit 5 whenever it occurs in a number. Thus 5, 10 and 15 should all be pronounced 'buzz' and 50 and 51 should be pronounced 'buzzty' and 'buzzty-one'; 55 is 'buzzty-buzz'.

If Fizz is being played, then 7 is the forbidden number, not 5, and the word 'fizz' is substituted. So it goes one, two, three, four, five, six, fizz, eight, nine, ten, eleven, twelve, thirteen, fizz, fifteen through to fizzty-fizz (77) and beyond.

Buzz-Fizz (believe it or not) is a combination of Buzz and Fizz. So for example, 57 becomes 'buzzty-fizz' and 75 becomes 'fizzty-buzz'.

You may, if you wish, switch from Fizz to Buzz to Buzz-Fizz in the course of a game, just to make it more confusing.

Any player who says a number instead of fizzing (or vice versa) or who fizzes when he should buzz (or vice versa) drops out of the game.

The last player left is the winner.

Coffee Pot

One player thinks of a word that has two meanings (e.g. duck) or a pair of words that have different meanings but which sound the same (e.g. bored and board). Then she speaks a sentence out loud using both meanings but substituting the words 'coffee pot' for both of them.

For example, 'If you see a low-flying coffee pot you'd better coffee pot', or 'I was on the coffee pot but I quit because I got so coffee pot.'

Each of the other players may then ask one question, and the first player's answer must include one or other of his words, again disguised as 'coffee pot'.

For example the question might be, 'What did you do today?' and the reply might be, 'I went to the shops and bought a coffee pot to roast for my dinner.'

If one of the players manages to identify the 'coffee pot' word, he scores a point and it is his turn to have a go at being the 'coffee potter'. If no one manages to guess, the current 'coffee potter' scores a point and comes up with another 'coffee pot'.

The player who finishes with the most points is the winner.

Fingers

This is a guessing game that's perfect for keeping those in the back seat busy. The aim is to guess the total number of fingers (from nought to ten) that will be displayed by two players. Each player conceals one hand behind his or her back. Simultaneously they both show their other hand with any number of fingers extended. For the purposes of this game, thumbs count as fingers and a clenched fist represents nought. At the same time as revealing their hand, each player calls out a number from nought to ten, which is their guess at the total number of fingers that will be displayed. If both players guess correctly, or if neither guesses correctly, the round is a draw.

Any previously agreed number of rounds may be played.

Heard not Seen

This is a marvellous game to play after you've had a rowdy round of Buzz-Fizz (page 57) and feel like something a little calmer. It tends to be a big hit with the older members of our particular band of merry travellers as it requires *complete* quiet.

All you do is sit back and listen in silence for five whole minutes. As you listen you can write down (or *remember*, if writing on the move makes you carsick and you've got a good memory) all the sounds you can hear. When the time's up the player with the longest list wins.

You probably think that there isn't much to hear sitting in silence inside a car, but you'd be wrong, and here's a list of very common sounds to prove it:

The wind
An aeroplane flying overhead
The screech of brakes
An ambulance or fire engine or police car siren
A car horn
A car radio
Birdsong
A clock striking
A train
A pneumatic drill

Saethryd says: For those of you of a spiritual bent, think of this game as a chance to bring out your inner Buddhist. Rather than writing down, recording or remembering the sounds, turn the game into an exercise in mindfulness – a literal moving meditation. Listen, focus on the sounds, clear the mind, turn on, tune in and drop out, and by the time you come off the M5 you'll be as blissed out as the Dalai Lama on the road to Mandalay.

'I like apples . . .'

This game works well in a packed people carrier or minibus to Margate. You can only play it once. The longer it takes for the last player to cotton on while everyone else has worked it out, the more fun it is.

You start the game by telling your passengers a list of the things you do and don't like:

> I like apples, but I don't like oranges;
> I like football, but I don't like cricket;
> I like food, but I don't like drink;
> I like trees, but I don't like flowers;
> I like doors, but I don't like windows;
> I like Leeds and Liverpool, but I don't like London.

Have you worked out yet what's special about those particular likes and dislikes? Well, all the things 'I like' contain two vowels or two consonants right next to each other — aPPles, fOOtball, fOOd, trEEs, dOOrs, LEEds, LiverpOOl — and all the things 'I don't like' don't.

As soon as a fellow passenger catches on to this, she interrupts you and tells you what she likes and dislikes. If you know she's got the idea — because she tells you she likes yeLLow but doesn't like pink or because she likes HoLLand but doesn't like France — you may declare 'I like *you*' and she can join in listing likes and dislikes for the still befuddled other players. The last person to catch on to the idea is the loser.

'I packed my bag ...'

This is the world-famous memory game in which the players have to keep track of an ever-lengthening list of items.

The first player begins by saying, 'I packed my bag and in it I put ... my toothbrush.'

The second player then says, 'I packed my bag and in it I put ... my toothbrush and brown shoes.'

The third player continues, 'I packed my bag and in it I put ... my toothbrush, brown shoes and my copy of *Alice in Wonderland*.'

And so it goes on around the group until someone forgets an item in the list or gets it in the wrong order, at which point that player has to drop out and the others continue without him.

The last player left packing his bag is the winner.

'If I had a million pounds . . .'

If you had a million pounds, how would you spend it? Would you spend it all on sports cars or sweets? Investments or ice cream? Would you give it away and if you did, who would you give it to? There's no more entertaining way of spending a journey from Wigan to Wilmslow (or Washington, County Durham, to Washington, DC) than by working out how you would spend your wonga. Here's one list of ideas:

One small castle in Scotland	£145,000.00
One small aeroplane	£62,000.00
One Rolls-Royce motor car	£23,000.00
One motor-bike	£500.00
One gold-plated pogo stick	£100.00
Luxury holiday in Australia	£2,400.00
Ocean racing yacht	£170,000.00
Presents to parents	£200,000.00
Presents to siblings	£300,000.00
Supply of ice cream for life	£2,000.00
Large stable and 20 ponies	£45,000.00
Indoor heated swimming pool	£5,000.00
Supply of roast beef and Yorkshire pudding for life	£10,000.00
Private cinema	£34,000.00

Grand banquet for 100 guests	£900.00
Pedigree pussy cat	£95.00
De luxe Scrabble set	£5.00

Total = £1,000,000.00

Now how would you spend *your* million?

Saethryd says: It should be noted that Dad started working on this list when he was about Rory's age and it hasn't changed much since. Hence the gold-plated pogo stick and the grand banquet at nine pounds a head – a veritable bargain! (Though I am tempted to find out how much a lifetime supply of roast beef and Yorkshire pudding is retailing at these days . . .)

Gyles says: Wait a moment, Saethryd. The curse of inflation has encroached on everything since I was a young man (with hair! and hopes!). I think we need to face reality on this one and update my spending spree on the following basis:

One small castle in Scotland	£2,900,000.00
One small aeroplane	£4,800,000.00
One Rolls-Royce motor car	£300,000.00
One motor-bike	£11,000.00
One gold-plated pogo stick	£3,000.00
Luxury holiday in Australia	£12,000.00
Ocean racing yacht	£7,000,000.00

Presents to parents (actually repayment of assorted loans)	£30,000.00
Presents to siblings (sorry, folks, times are tough)	£3,000.00
Supply of ice cream for life	£30,000.00
Large stable and 20 ponies	£900,000.00
Indoor heated swimming pool	£150,000.00
Supply of roast beef and Yorkshire pudding for life	£15,000.00
Private cinema	£135,000.00
Grand banquet for 100 guests	£25,000.00
Pedigree pussy cat	£500.00
De luxe Scrabble set	£150.00

So, these days, it seems it's the £16,314,650 game.

Sausages

O ne of the players is chosen to be the questioner. He may ask any of the other players whatever personal questions he might choose, such as 'What do you think your legs look like?', 'What are you shoes made from?' or 'To what do you attribute your wit and vitality?' Whatever the question, the player being asked must reply 'Sausages'. The first player who smiles or laughs or smirks or giggles or titters or grins or chortles or simpers or guffaws or sniggers, or otherwise betrays any emotion other than deadly seriousness, is out, and he takes the next turn at being questioner.

Tennis, Elbow, Foot

Each player in turn calls out a word which is either directly associated with the word previously called out or which rhymes with it. For example:

Tennis

Elbow

Foot

Ball

Wall

Paper

Tiger

Stripe

Ripe

Fruit

Apple

Core

Door

Key

Note

Boat . . .

And so on.

Players are out if they hesitate, if they repeat a word already called out, or if they call out a word which neither relates to the previous word nor rhymes with it. The last player left in is the winner.

This is a tricky game to play.

Swimming
Pool
Cool
Dude
Rude
Nude
Naked
Gun
Fun
Game
Set
Match . . .

Ooops! Whoever said 'Match' is out, because it follows on from 'Game and Set' together, but on its own it does not really follow on from 'Set'. 'Vet' or 'Net' or 'Bet', or 'Down' or 'Off', would have worked, but 'Match' doesn't.

Word Associations

The first player says the first word that comes into her mind. The second player immediately says the first word that comes into his mind in response the first player's word. The third player responds likewise to the second player's word, and so on round and round the car. If a player hesitates before saying his word he is out. The last player left in is the winner. This game is sometimes called Psychotherapy, and psychiatrists may charge very high fees for playing it with you.

OBSERVATION GAMES

• • •

You're stuck in the car, wedged in the middle seat between Aunty Ginny and cousin Ciara's (slightly weird) new boyfriend. Your body may be trapped but your eyes can still gaze out the windows and soak in the glorious freedom of the open road (or the M3, whatever you want to call it). Here are some classic observation games, to help bring the outside in.

Driving Blind

The very first of our observation games and there's no actual observing going on . . . in fact, your eyes are shut the whole time. Oh, the irony! But that is the topsy-turvy world we inhabit here at Brandreth Towers; and, no, the object of the game is not to see how far you can drive with your eyes shut!

In fact, the driver is not allowed to play at all: she must simply choose a visible object in the distance (a service station or a church or a village or a flyover) and persuade her passengers to close *their* eyes and only open them when they think they have reached the given object. The player who opens his eyes at the point when the car is nearest the object scores a point. The first player to score 10 points is the winner.

If you are a stickler for accuracy, the variation that follows could more legitimately be described as an observation game . . .

Mile's End

The aim of this game is to guess when you have travelled exactly one mile. At a certain moment the driver calls out 'Start!', and as soon after that as you think you have travelled a mile you shout 'Now!' The player who shouts 'Now!' nearest to the right moment is the winner.

'First one to spot . . .'

This game is fantastic for keeping eyes peeled and mouths closed in hushed concentration.

The driver always goes first and begins the game by choosing an object for the passengers to spot – a post box, a dog, a woman in a hat, a double-decker bus, a house with a blue door. The item chosen should be tricky enough that it won't be immediately spotted, but not so obscure that it takes hours before the car passes one.

The first person to spot the object calls out (in our experience, loudly and with great excitement), points to the object and gets to choose the next item to be spotted.

A deceptively simple game, 'First one to spot . . .' is surprisingly engaging. We once spent the entire journey from Hampstead to Hammersmith scouring the streets of London for a sausage dog. And it's particularly fun to play around Christmas time, when you can add snowmen, inflatable Father Christmases and all sorts of festive objects to the list.

Rory says: I love this game.

Treasure Hunt: 'Got it!', 'Bingo!', 'I'm wearing trousers made of cheese'

This game is a variation of 'First one to spot . . .' Here, rather than looking for one object at time, before the journey begins a list is compiled of up to ten objects. Each passenger is given the list and must cross the objects off one by one as they spot them. The winner is the first player to spot all the items on the list and to shout 'Got it!' or 'Bingo!' or whatever phrase has been previously agreed. Getting the phrase right is important in case of a tie. (Our family phrases include 'Sausage!', 'Goody goody gumdrops!' and 'I'm wearing trousers made of cheese'.)

'I Spy'

There cannot be many people who have never played a round of 'I Spy'. The game is a true classic and the perfect introduction to the wonderful world of observation games. Just in case you've been missing out, here's how it is played.

A player thinks of an object that is visible in or from the car – a tractor, for example – and announces to the other players its initial by saying, 'I spy with my little eye something beginning with T.' The other players then have to guess what it is.

Question: Tree?
Answer: No.
Question: Train track?
Answer: No.
Question: Telephone wires?
Answer: No.
Question: Uncle Trevor?
Answer: No!!
Question: Toffees?
Answer: No.

And so it goes on . . . The first player to guess correctly is allowed to spy the next object.

Marking Makers

Each player chooses a make of car – Ford, Honda, Volkswagen, Jaguar, Toyota, Mercedes, Rover, Skoda, Rolls-Royce, Kia – and over a set period of time, say fifteen minutes, half an hour, or even the entire journey, tries to spot as many of their make as they can. When the time is up, the player who has collected most cars is the winner.

NUMBER PLATE GAMES

• • •

Cars have had number plates in Great Britain since 1 January 1904 and people have been using them to play games ever since. Here's a selection our favourites.

Number Plate Numbers

The aim of the game is to count from 1 to 20 and to do so by spotting all twenty figures on the number plates of passing cars. The first player to spot each number gets it. When you've got 1 (from R61 BDV, EN17 RZZ or F31 PQQ) you can move on to 2 (which you'll find in L62 FRD, B24 PHY, and T12 GYV) and then 3, and so on. You can only get one number from each number plate (so P12 XYZ will give you 1 *or* 2 *or* 12 but not all three) and when you get into double figures (from 10 to 20) the two figures you want must come side by side in the right order (so S10 TGB will give you 10 but S01 TGB won't).

The first player to get to 20 wins.

Number Plate Letters

You play this game in exactly the same way as you play Number Plate Numbers, but you use the letters in the number plates you pass instead. If it's a long journey, use all the letters in the alphabet and work your way from A to Z. If you're on a short trip, leave out the Q. (Qs are not very common on number plates, and waiting for a car with a Q can bring the game to a grinding halt.)

Number Plate Messages

The driver gives each player in turn a different number plate and the player has to turn the letters in his number plate into a special message. Anyone who can't think of a message drops out. The last player left giving out messages is the winner.

It sounds trickier than it is, so here are some examples.

ABC could be:
Armed Bandits Coming
Air-force Bans Chocolate
Ark Boards Camels
Ant Bites Cockroach
Abel Beats Cain

FSU could be:
Free Sally's Uncle
False Start Underway
Friends Stand Up
Flying Saucer Unidentified
Football Supporters United

Sentence Search

S imilar to Number Plate Letters, this game requires keeping the car windows spotlessly clean so you can be sure to see every passing car.

To play, everyone has to choose a sentence or phrase consisting of exactly eight letters. Here are some examples:

OFF YOU GO

CATS PLAY

YOU ARE HE

BAD BILLY

GO ON JOHN

I LOVE HER

Now what you do is race to see who can spot the letters to complete their sentence or phrase first. You can take the letters from anywhere in the number plate, but you can't take a letter that somebody else has already spotted and you must spot the letters in the correct order.

The first player to have spelt his phrase or sentence is the winner. (And if you want to win, don't choose 'I LOVE HER' as your eight-letter phrase. The letter I is like the letter Q. It does not turn up on car number plates that often.)

Sum It Up

Players take it in turn to adopt the passing cars and add up the figures on the number plates. For example, ABC 957 adds up to 21 and XYZ 1046 adds up to 11. The aim of the game is to be the first player whose sum total of car numbers adds up to exactly 50. 51, 52, 53 won't do: it must be 50. Anyone overshooting the mark has to start again at zero.

Traffic Census

This is a game to play when you are parked in a lay-by and can see the traffic travelling in both directions. The players divide into two teams and one team watches the vehicles going in one direction and the other team watches the vehicles going in another direction. Each team scores points for the vehicles they see, and the team with the highest score at the end of the set period has won. Here's how you score:

Four-door car	1
Two-door car	2
Van	3
Lorry with four wheels	3
Lorry with more than four wheels	4
Coach	4
Double-decker bus	4
Motor-bike	5
Bicycle	6
Caravan	7
Convertible with the roof down	7
Horse-drawn vehicle	50

Twenty Questions

Probably *the* classic car journey game. Here are our versions.

Animal, Vegetable, Mineral

O ne of the world's best-known and most loved word games, Twenty Questions started life in the nineteenth century as a popular parlour game. In the twentieth century it became an even more popular radio and television panel game. Who knows what awaits it in the twenty-first . . .

To play the Animal, Vegetable, Mineral version, one player thinks of an object – it can be anything from an apple to a zebra; from Mickey Mouse to the M4. When he has something in mind, he has to declare whether what he is thinking of is 'Animal', 'Vegetable' or 'Mineral' (or any combination of the three). If the object is a pony, then, obviously, it is 'Animal'; if it's a pony and trap, it is 'Animal and Mineral (possibly with Vegetable connections if you think it might be used to take the farmer's cabbages to market)'. The other players, in turn, ask any questions they like, provided that the questions can be answered by a simple 'Yes' or 'No' ('Does it have four legs?', 'Can you eat it?', 'Is there one in the house right now?'), the aim being to narrow down the field and eventually identify the mystery object.

If the object has not been identified when twenty questions have been asked, then the player who thought of the object in question reveals to the other players what it is. He then selects another object for them to identify. If any player correctly identifies the mystery object, then that player is given the privilege of selecting the next object.

Saethryd says: Here is an alternative version of this game, which I was taught by my friend Piers on a long car journey back from Hereford. We found it most enjoyable.

It is essentially exactly the same as Twenty Questions (Animal, Vegetable, Mineral), but you have to be thinking of something that has a connection to fish. It can be obvious – fish fingers – it can be obscure – one of the little ceramic divers you find in a fishtank – it can be really obscure – Michael Fish, the weatherman – but it *has* to be fish-related. Why? Who knows? I save my questions for the game . . .

Colourful

In this version of Twenty Questions, one player thinks of an object and tells the other players the colour of the object. They then ask up to twenty questions to try and find out what the object is, but can only be given 'Yes' or 'No' answers. Every time a 'Yes' answer is given, the player who asked the particular question can have a guess at the object. Here's an easy example:

Player: My colour is blue.
Question 1: Can you wear it?
Answer: No.
Question 2: Can you touch it?
Answer: No.
Question 3: Can you see it from the car?
Answer: Yes.
Question 4: Is it that blue Jaguar in front of us?
Answer: No.
Question 5: Is it a long way away?
Answer: Yes.
Question 6: Is it the sea?
Answer: No.
Question 7: Is it very big?
Answer: Yes.

Question 8: Is it the large road sign we saw as we came on to the motorway?

Answer: No.

Question 9: Is it above us?

Answer: Yes.

Question 10: Is it the sky?

Answer: Yes!

The player who guesses what the object is can choose the next object.

Gyles says: We weren't in the United Kingdom when we played this game or the sky would scarcely have been blue. We were in Spain. Oh, yes. *Olé!*

Hide and Seek

No, this isn't a game where you have to hide in the footwell or put a blanket over your head while your fellow passengers count to twenty and then attempt to find you. It's a talking game where one player has to 'hide' himself in London – or Paris or Rome or Swansea or New York or where you've just been, or where you are going to, or any town or city you and the other players know well – and the rest have to find out where he is by asking him questions. He can only give 'Yes' or 'No' answers and only twenty questions are allowed. The questioner who guesses where the player is hiding is the next one to hide. If no one guesses before the twenty questions have been asked, then the hider is allowed to hide himself somewhere else. Here's an example set in London:

> Question 1: Are you in an Underground station?
> Answer: No.
> Question 2: Are you in a railway station?
> Answer: No.
> Question 3: Are you near the Houses of Parliament?
> Answer: No.
> Question 4: Are you near the River Thames?
> Answer: Yes.
> Question 5: Are you south of the river?

Answer: No.

Question 6: Are you in a public building?

Answer: Yes.

Question 7: Is it a very large building?

Answer: Yes.

Question 8: Is it a very old building?

Answer: Yes.

Question 9: Is it a church or cathedral?

Answer: No.

Question 10: Is it a castle or palace?

Answer: Yes.

Question 11: Are you hiding in the Tower of London?

Answer: Yes!

'What's my name?'

One player chooses to be a famous fictional character, for example from a book or a play or a film or a television series, and the other players must try to find out who he is by asking him twenty questions, which he must answer as he thinks the character would. For example, if you were being Popeye and you were asked what you had eaten for breakfast, you would answer 'Spinach'.

Can you guess from these questions and answers the name of the next character?

Question 1: What did you do today?

Answer: I had a very busy day. I had to fight with some pirates.

Question 2: What do you like doing best?

Answer: Flying

Question 3: What do you hate doing most?

Answer: Going to bed.

Question 4: What are you going to do when you grow up?

Answer: I am not going to grow up.

Question 5: Do you live alone?

Answer: No, I live with lots of other boys. I'm their leader.

Question 6: Where do you live?

Answer: On an island.

Question 7: Aren't there any girls on the island?

Answer: There's one that comes to visit me every year. She flies all the way from London to help me do my spring cleaning.

The first player to guess that the character's name is Peter Pan gets the chance to choose the next mystery character.

'Who am I?'

One player chooses to be somebody; it can be anybody, a character from fact or fiction, Horatio Nelson or Winnie the Pooh, Florence Nightingale or Britney Spears, Spiderman or Barack Obama, so long as it is somebody of whom all the players are likely to have heard. The player then gives the others the first letter of the mystery person's name and they then ask her twenty questions in their attempt to find out who she is. She can only give 'Yes' or 'No' answers and whoever manages to guess who she is gets the chance to be the next mystery person. If nobody guesses, then the player has another turn. Here's an example:

Player: I am someone beginning with V. Who am I?

Question 1: Are you fact?

Answer: Yes.

Question 2: Are you alive?

Answer: No.

Question 3: Are you a man?

Answer: No.

Question 4: Are you British?

Answer: Yes.

Question 5: Are you modern?

Answer: No.

Question 6: Are you from the nineteenth century?

Answer: Yes.

Question 7: Are you a writer?

Answer: No.

Question 8: Are you a scientist?

Answer: No.

Question 9: Are you an entertainer?

Answer: No.

Question 10: Are you married?

Answer: Yes.

Question 11: Do you have several children?

Answer: Yes.

Question 12: Are you a member of the royal family?

Answer: Yes.

Question 13: Are you Queen Victoria?

Answer: Yes!

ANALOGUE Fun in a Digital WORLD

If you look in on a family pub today – or look around the fast-food diner – or look across the bus – you might be forgiven for wondering what on earth parents did to keep their children occupied before the advent of the handy smartphone.

Well, truth will out. Before the age of the tablet and the mobile, children played games – but not wearing earphones and not on screens. And some of the best of the games they played feature in this chapter, with volume levels down, fun levels up, brain cells multiplying and no danger of repetitive strain injury or the dreaded Square Eyes. (Mark our words, kids, it will *happen if you stare at a screen too long. You should see the state of Rory's poor old cousin Maise – a terrible case of the Goggle Boxes.)*

Most of these games require no more than two players, a piece of paper and a couple of pencils. At the very most, you will need a box of matches and a few coins, nothing that can't be found in your pocket, at the bottom of your bag or behind the bar.

We hummed and hawed over doing a Pippa and including some of the more obvious and better-known games, but decided that if we could introduce just one poor games-deprived soul to the joys of Noughts and Crosses, then it would all have been worth it.

From the strategies of Battleships to the intellectual demands of Word Squares and the surreal humour of Consequences, this selection of on-the-go games should delight and entertain children and adults alike.

Definitely no Wi-Fi required!

PENCIL-AND-PAPER GAMES

• • •

Aggression

Aggression is a pencil-and-paper war game in which two players attack and conquer each other's countries. The objective is to reduce as far as possible the number of countries occupied by an opponent's armies while trying to retain as many as possible of the countries occupied by one's own armies. Players can cast themselves in the role of Napoleon versus Wellington or Montgomery versus Rommel or America versus just about anyone – or even, if they prefer, Julius Caesar with his legions versus Genghis Khan with his Tatar hordes.

This game is also a good example of a simple-but-complex game, in that it can be easily learnt and played at a basic level by children, or it can be played by professors of mathematics with considerable in-depth analysis of strategy and tactics.

The first stage is the drawing of the battle area, which is a map of a number of imaginary countries with common boundaries. Any number of countries may be drawn, but twenty is the usual number. They may be any size and shape, but should not be too small. The players take it in turn when drawing the map, each adding one country in his or her turn. The countries are then marked with letters for identification.

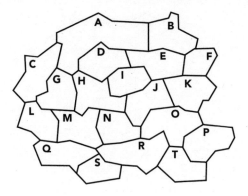

The second stage of the game is to occupy the countries with armies. Each player has 100 armies. The players take it in turn to allocate any number of their armies to an unoccupied country, writing the number of armies in the appropriate area. For example, player one may decide to occupy country D with 20 of his armies, then player two may decide to occupy J with 22 armies, then player one may put 3 armies in A, and so on. Preferably, pencils of two different colours should be used to distinguish player one from player two; alternatively, a player may underline their numbers.

It is for each player to decide whether to occupy a few countries with large numbers of armies, or whether to place a few armies in each of a large number of countries.

This stage of the game finishes when both players have allocated all their armies, or when all the countries have been occupied.

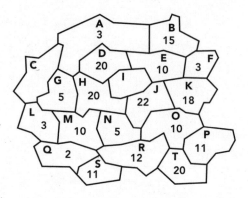

The third and final stage of the game is the aggressive part. Each player in turn uses the armies in one or more of the countries they have occupied to conquer an adjacent country occupied by their opponent, thus wiping out the opponent's armies stationed in that country. Adjacent countries are those with a common boundary. For example, in the game illustrated here A, E and F are adjacent to B, and E, F, J and O are all adjacent to K.

A player may conquer a country held by their opponent only if he has more armies in adjacent countries than the opponent has in the country being attacked. The number of armies in the conquered country is crossed out, playing no further part in the game. The conquering armies, however, remain intact.

It should be noted that conquering a country does not increase the number of countries that a player occupies – it simply decreases the number of countries occupied by the opponent. Countries not occupied by either player take no part in this stage of the game except as neutral zones.

The game ends when neither player can conquer any more countries. The player with the most countries is the winner. The game illustrated might proceed this way:

Player one	*Player two*
A, E, F conquer B	P, R conquer T
A, D conquer H	J conquers K
O conquers N	R conquers S
A, L conquer G	J conquers O
(Player 1 passes as he cannot	
conquer any more countries)	J conquers E
	M conquers L
	M conquers Q

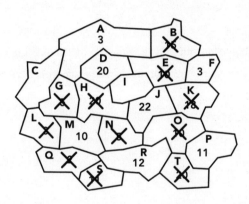

Player two wins since he has four countries left while player one is left with only three.

All Ways

This game can be played by as many people as are up for the challenge. Everyone will need a pencil and a piece of paper.

Choose a long word – any long word will do – and get the players to write it in the centre of their pieces of paper, like this:

UMBRELLA

Players then have two minutes to build up as many other words as they can from the basic word. All the new words must in some way be related to the first word, like this:

```
                s
    s           q
    t           u
c o l d         a
    r           l   g
U M B R E L L   A
    a           l
    i           o
r a i n         s o a k e d
    c           h         r
    o           e         e
  d a m p       s         n
    t                     c
                          h
                          e
                        d r o w n e d
```

When the time's up, the player with the most words wins.

Alphabet Race

This is a two-player game.

Each player needs a pencil and a piece of paper; a third piece of paper is placed on the table between the players and acts as the 'board'.

Before beginning play, each player should list the twenty-six letters of the alphabet on his own piece of paper.

Once play begins, the first player writes a word on the board and, when he's written it, he crosses off the letters he used from his alphabet. For example, if he begins by putting the word FIRST on the board he then crosses out the letters F, I, R, S and T, on his piece of paper.

His opponent now has to add a word to the board and then crosses off the letters he's used from his alphabet. For example, had the second player added ROOM to FIRST, the board would have looked like this:

$$F \quad I \quad R \quad S \quad T$$
$$O$$
$$O$$
$$M$$

and he would have been able to cross out the letters O and M from his alphabet. He would not have been able to cross out R because a player can only eliminate letters he actually plays, not those he merely builds upon.

The players take it in turn to put words on the board, crossing off the letters they have used each time. If a player cannot play, he can say 'Pass' and misses a turn. The first player to have crossed off all twenty-six letters from his alphabet is the winner. If both players say 'Pass' in succession, then the game ends automatically and the player with fewer letters left is the winner.

Battleships

L egend has it the game of Battleships was invented by British prisoners-of-war in Germany during the First World War. The French and Russians also lay claim to being its originators. All we know for sure is that it started gaining popularity as a game at the beginning of the 1920s; by the 1930s and 1940s pad-and-pencil editions were being made; in 1967 the first board-game version was released; and in the late 1970s it took on a new guise as one of the first computer games to be developed. Today it remains a very popular game, a true classic, which is just as enjoyable played the old-fashioned way with pencils and paper, skill and luck.

There are many versions of the game, the version described here being one of the simplest. Battleships is a game for two players, and each of you will need a pencil and piece of paper.

Life will be a bit easier if you happen to have some graph paper with preprinted squares, the kind you might find in a maths book. If not, it is not too much of a chore to take pencil in hand and draw two boards of ten squares by ten squares. The squares down the vertical side of each board are numbered and those along the horizontal side are lettered so that each square may be identified by its number and letter, for example A1, A2, A3, B1, B2, B3, and so on. Title the first board HOME FLEET and the second board ENEMY FLEET.

That sounds more complicated than it looks. It looks like this:

Home Fleet

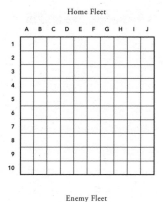

Enemy Fleet

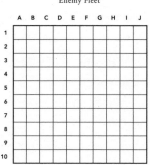

Now the battlefields are set and each player must deploy their navy on their HOME FLEET board. While this is done, and from here on in till the end of the game, each player must take care that his sheet cannot be seen by the other player.

Your navy consists of the following ships of the following sizes:

1 battleship (4 squares each)

2 cruisers (3 squares each)

3 destroyers (2 squares each)

4 submarines (1 square each)

A player may place ships where he likes on his HOME FLEET board using the following codes: D for destroyer, B for battleship, C for cruiser, S for submarine. This action is subject to the following two rules: (a) the squares forming each ship must be in a straight line, across or down; and (b) there must be at least one empty square between ships – in other words, no two ships may touch even at a corner.

Again it sounds more complicated than it is. Here is an example of how you might deploy your navy at the start of a game.

Home Fleet

	A	B	C	D	E	F	G	H	I	J
1										D
2										D
3			C	C	C		B			
4							B			
5							B			
6		C				S	B			
7		C		S						
8		C					D	D		
9				D	D					
10							S			

Enemy Fleet

	A	B	C	D	E	F	G	H	I	J
1										
2										
3										
4										
5										
6										
7										
8										
9										
10										

When both players have drawn their fleets, battle can commence. The objective, of course, is to sink the enemy fleet. Each player in turn fires a shot at the enemy fleet by naming a square out loud, for example A7 or D3.

The opponent then examines his Home Fleet area to see whether that square is occupied by a ship. He must declare whether the shot was a Hit or Miss, and if it was a Hit he must identify the type of ship. The player firing the shot records a Miss by marking the appropriate square on the ENEMY FLEET board with a dot, or he records a Hit by marking the square with a letter identifying the type of ship.

The players continue firing alternately until one of the players wins the game by completely destroying the enemy fleet.

Here's an example of a game in mid-battle:

Home Fleet

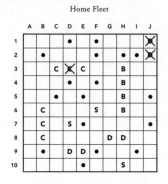

Enemy Fleet

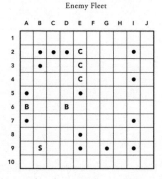

In the game illustrated it is clear that shots on squares B6 and C6 are required to sink the enemy battleship. It is also clear that, because of the rules as to the placing of the ships, squares such as D5, F2 and C9 must be unoccupied, so it would pointless to waste shots on them.

In other versions of the game, the size of the playing area or the number of each type of ship may be different from those described here. In some versions, too, ships may be placed diagonally as well as horizontally and vertically, and there may be no restriction on ships accompanying adjacent squares. Our advice is master the art of playing basic Battleships before you start on the convoluted variations.

Boxes

To play this classic pencil-and-paper game you will need . . . a piece of paper and a pencil. An opponent also comes in handy. Traditionally a two-player game, Boxes can be played with more if you fancy.

Start by drawing your board. It will consist of ten rows of ten dots and look like this:

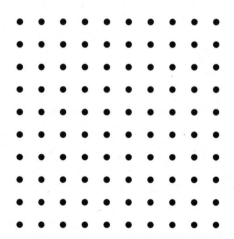

The aim of the game is to make as many 'boxes' as possible (the clue is in the name). The players take it in turn to draw a straight line connecting any two dots which are next to each other, either horizontally or vertically. Diagonal lines are not allowed. If you draw in the fourth line, the one which completes the 'box' or square, it is yours to claim. Write your initial inside it and take another turn. The game ends when all the boxes have been completed. The player who has captured the most squares at the end of the game is the victor.

In the game illustrated here (in which neither player has played very skilfully) the player whose turn it is next will be able to complete four boxes in the lower right-hand corner.

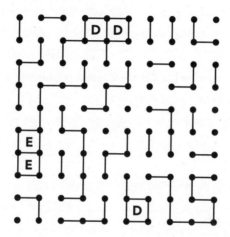

Gyles says: The game may begin with fewer dots if a quick game is required and with more if a longer game is wanted. Players who really enjoy Boxes don't restrict themselves to a paltry ten rows of ten dots. Oh no, they play on a *much* grander scale. A thousand rows with a thousand dots in each row is not unknown.

Consequences

This is one of the oldest of the evergreen parlour games. It remains as popular now as it was in Queen Victoria's day. Marvellously silly and played purely for amusement, it even inspired an art movement: the Surrealists, spearheaded by André Breton, used to play a version with the rather macabre title *Cadavres Exquis* (Exquisite Corpses) in the parlours and salons of 1920s Paris.

The idea of the game is to create little stories (or pictures) to which each player contributes a part without knowing what any of the other players has created. This random composition produces unexpected, often ludicrous and sometimes hilarious results.

Any number of players can play the game. Each player is provided with a pencil and a sheet of paper, and is then instructed to write down certain bits of entertaining information. After the players have finished writing they fold the top of their paper forward to cover up the writing. The folded piece of paper is then passed from player to player in clockwise fashion, so that each player simultaneously receives a different folded sheet from the player on their left. Each player adds a fresh piece of information to each sheet of paper, and these build up into a story, or rather as many stories as there are players, because each player started a story on their piece of paper.

At the end of the game all the stories are read out to the gleeful assembly.

The parts of the story may vary (you can do it your way), but the traditional Consequences story goes something like this:

1. *An adjective/description* e.g. **Blissful** (fold and pass)
2. *A female character* e.g. **Little Bo Peep** (fold and pass)
3. met *An adjective/description* e.g. **firm but fair** (fold and pass)
4. *A male character* e.g. **Andy Murray** (fold and pass)
5. *Where they met* e.g. **behind the bicycle shed** (fold and pass)
6. *What he did* e.g. **He declared his undying love** (fold and pass)
7. *What she did* e.g. **She danced like no one was watching** (fold and pass)
8. *What he said* e.g. **He said 'I couldn't half murder a kebab'** (fold and pass)
9. *What she said* e.g. **She said 'You're fired'** (fold and pass)
10. *What the consequence was* e.g. **The consequence was a devastating earthquake** (fold and pass)
11. *What the world said* e.g. **And the world said, 'It is better to have loved and lost than never to have loved at all.'**

Picture Consequences

They say a picture is worth a thousand words, so why not test out the theory with this version of Consequences geared to the more artistically inclined? This is also the version to play with the younger crowd, who may still be mastering their ABCs. A few giggles are guaranteed.

Each player is given a pencil and a sheet of paper which has two lines drawn across it to divide the paper into three equal sections. The lines are not absolutely necessary but they do make the game easier for young children.

In the top section the players draw a head or face – it can be a silly face, a sad face, the head of a bird, an animal, an alien from the planet Zog. It doesn't matter, so long as the player doesn't let anyone else see what she is drawing. The neck should be drawn to go just over the line and into the middle section. When the heads have been drawn all the players fold down their pieces of paper so as to cover up the faces and then pass the pieces of paper to the players sitting on their right. Everyone then has to draw a body and some arms (or wings!) and the tops of legs just peeking over the second line. This done, they again fold over the paper to cover what they have drawn and pass the paper on to whoever is sitting on their right, who completes the picture. When all the pictures are completed, fold one final time and then pass around for the players to unfold the sheets to see what has been drawn and laugh themselves silly.

Rory says: I love this game.

Crossing Out the Letters

This is a marvellous game to play when you are out and about at a restaurant or café and are looking for something to keep the kids busy for a few minutes. Give each player a page from a newspaper and tell them that on the command, 'Go!', they have got to cross out all the letters A (or B or C or X or Y or Z) that they can find on the page. The aim of the game is to have crossed out more of the letters than any other player within a set period of time.

To make the game completely fair, you should buy as many copies of the same newspaper as you will have players, so that each player can be given exactly the same sheet of newspaper. To make it even more complicated, you can get the players not only to cross out one letter, but also to cross out certain words – like 'and' and 'at' or 'or' and 'but'.

Hangman

In this popular game one player thinks of a word, preferably of six or more letters, and the other player has to guess what it is.

Player one writes down a series of dashes to indicate the number of letters in the word, like this:

_ _ _ _ _ _ _

Player two then starts guessing the letters in the word, calling out one letter at a time. If the letter occurs in the word, player one writes that letter above the appropriate dash (or dashes) wherever it occurs, like this:

_ a_ _ _ a_

For each letter called out which does not occur in the word player one draws a part of the Hangman picture in the following order:

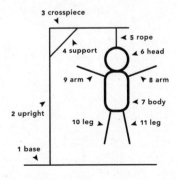

1. Base
2. Upright
3. Crosspiece
4. Support
5. Rope
6. Head
7. Body
8. Arm
9. Arm
10. Leg
11. Leg

The incorrectly guessed letters are also recorded underneath the dashes so that player two can see which letters have already been tried.

Player two wins if he or she correctly guesses the word or all the letters in the word before the picture is completed and the man is 'hanged'. The winner gets to be the hangman for the next round and chooses the word for the other player to guess.

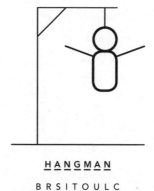

H A N G M A N
B R S I T O U L C

If the picture is completed before player two has identified all the letters, then player one stays on as hangman and chooses another word.

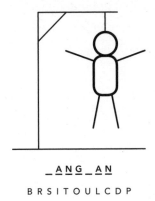

_ A N G _ A N

B R S I T O U L C D P

Sometimes the game is played using agreed themes, such as Book Titles or Pop Stars, in which case the name or title to be guessed may be more than one word. In this case, player one will draw the dashes to show the number of letters in each word with spaces between the words.

Saethryd says: A little tip for you. In case you didn't know, the most commonly used letters in the English language are e, t, a, o, i, n, s, h, r, d, l, u. Try them out first and you should be well on your way to victory. Call it strategy, call it cheating or just do what I do and call it WINNING! (But if anyone asks, you didn't hear it from me.)

Gyles says: We Brandreths takes a peculiar personal interest in this game because we have a forebear who was hanged. Jeremiah Brandreth (1790–1817) was an out-of-work stocking-maker from Sutton-in-Ashfield in Nottinghamshire and a would-be revolutionary. Known as 'the hopeless radical', he hoped to overthrow the government of the day and 'end poverty forever'. He was to lead a group of men from Nottingham to join fifty thousand others in London and march on the Tower of London. The planned insurrection was foiled by the king's troops and Jeremiah and two co-conspirators were hanged and then beheaded. They were the last men in England to be beheaded for treason. When we Brandreths play Hangman, it's more than just a game: it's personal.

Joining Points

The players begin by marking any number of dots on a piece of paper. (Not too many or the game will go on forever). The players then take turns to join the dots together with lines that go from one dot to another without crossing themselves or each other. Only one line is allowed to join two dots and each dot can only have two lines leading from it.

The first player who is unable to draw a line is the loser.

Noughts and Crosses
(aka Tic Tac Toe or OXO)

There can't be many people in this world who haven't played a game of Noughts and Crosses. This tremendously popular children's game is a perennial favourite, which, for generations of schoolchildren, has been one of the principal means of relieving the tedium of boring lessons. Before play begins a framework is drawn consisting of two parallel lines crossing at right angles.

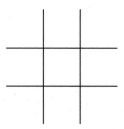

The players play alternately, the first player drawing a nought (circle) and the second player drawing a cross, in any one of the nine spaces that is vacant. The aim of the first player is to complete a row of three noughts, and the aim of the second player is to complete a row of three crosses. At the same time each player tries to block his or her opponent.

The winner is the first player to complete a row horizontally, vertically or diagonally.

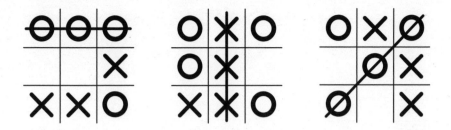

Once one learns the simple strategy required for this game it is impossible to lose unless one makes an absolutely appalling blunder. Between two experienced players every game will end in a draw, with neither player being able to complete a row.

Salvo

This game is similar to Battleships (page 109) but with one difference, which makes it a considerably more skilful game. The difference is that instead of firing one shot in his turn, a player fires a 'salvo' of three shots. The opponent then declares whether any of the shots were direct hits and what types of ship were hit by the salvo, but not the results of any individual shot. For example, the first player may call out 'C7, D12 and H2' and the second player may reply 'Two hits, one on a submarine and one on a battleship'.

The fact that the player does not know exactly which of his shots were hits makes this a more complex game than Battleships.

Shooting Stars

For this two-player game you will need a sheet of paper divided equally into three areas. One player has the top area, the other has the bottom area and the space in between is No Man's Land.

Before beginning to play, each player must position ten small circles wherever he likes within his own area. Along the front line of his area he must also position one small cross. Once the sheet of paper is looking something like this, the game can begin.

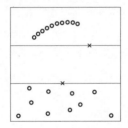

Starting from his own cross, each player now takes it in turn to draw a straight, short, sharp line right across No Man's Land into his opponent's area. If the line he draws goes through his opponent's area without touching any of the opponent's little circles, the player scores a point. If the line does touch any of the circles, then it is the opponent who scores the point. The first player to score 5 points is the winner.

This is one of those games that is much more exciting when played than when described, and it calls for considerably more skill than you would imagine.

Sprouts

S prouts was conceived in Cambridge in the early 1960s and so enthralling and ingenious a game is it that it has since spread throughout the world. Although the rules are simple, mastery of the game calls for skill and concentration.

You begin by marking three, four, five or more dots at random on a piece of paper. Players now take it in turn to draw a line joining any two of the dots or joining a dot to itself. When a player has drawn her line joining two dots, or drawn her loop joining a dot to itself, she must make a new dot somewhere along the line she has just drawn and then it is her opponent's turn. The opponent must also join any two dots or make a loop joining a dot to itself and then mark a new dot somewhere along the line he has just drawn.

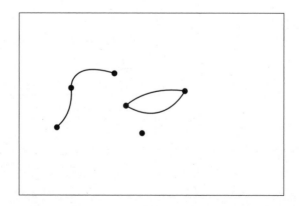

In drawing their lines and marking their dots, the players must remember two rules: (Rule 1) when drawing a line or a loop a player must not let it cross itself nor any other line that has already been drawn; and (Rule 2) no dot can have more than three lines leading from it.

The game continues with the players drawing their lines and adding dots to the lines they have drawn until one of the players cannot play. That player is the loser. The winner is the player who is able to draw the last line.

For example, in the position illustrated below, the player with the next turn must win. The only line that can be drawn will connect the top and bottom dots and, even though a new dot will be created on that line, it will be impossible to draw any further lines.

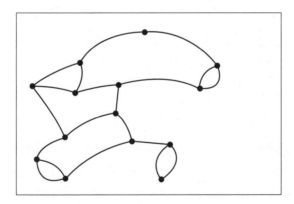

Word Squares

Word Squares is the *ideal* way to while away an afternoon among the logophiles you know and love.

For anyone fascinated by words, and there are quite a few of us out there, creating word squares is among the most absorbing of all time-wasters. The idea is simply to form a square of different words reading the same vertically as horizontally.

Squares involving three-, four- and five-letter words are relatively simple. Here is an example:

P L A Y
L O R E
A R E A
Y E A R

Devising squares with six-, seven- and eight-letter words is much more difficult, while creating a square with nine-letter words is well-nigh impossible (although it can be done, if you have an incredible vocabulary and an outsize dictionary). One man who has both is a Brandreth family friend, Darryl Francis, one of the world's leading authorities on Word Squares, and this is one of his favourite nine-letter wonders:

```
F  R  A  T  E  R  I  E  S
R  E  G  I  M  E  N  A  L
A  G  I  T  A  T  I  V  E
T  I  T  A  N  I  T  E  S
E  M  A  N  A  T  I  S  T
R  E  T  I  T  R  A  T  E
I  N  I  T  I  A  T  O  R
E  A  V  E  S  T  O  N  E
S  L  E  S  T  E  R  E  D
```

Darryl has some 999 others in the same vein. And that's not all; besides word squares in English, he turns out squares in Italian, Spanish, Icelandic and Esperanto.

Here is a French one he concocted on the bus the other day:

```
G  R  A  V  A  T  I  E  R
R  E  F  I  N  A  N  C  E
A  F  F  R  O  N  T  A  T
V  I  R  O  N  N  E  R  A
A  N  O  N  N  A  N  T  S
T  A  N  N  A  N  T  E  S
I  N  T  E  N  T  E  R  A
E  C  A  R  T  E  R  A  I
R  E  T  A  S  S  A  I  T
```

Staggering but it *can* be done and it is fun trying.

The Worm

This is a two-player game in a similar vein to our beloved Boxes (page 114).

To begin, ten rows of ten dots are marked on a sheet of paper, like this:

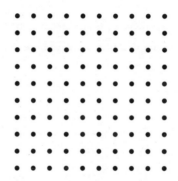

The first player draws a horizontal or vertical line to join any two adjacent dots. Diagonal lines are not allowed. The second player then draws another line, connecting either end of the existing line horizontally or vertically to any adjacent dot.

The players then continue playing alternately in this manner, drawing a line from either end of the existing line ('the worm') to an adjacent dot. The objective is to force one's opponent into a position in which he has to draw a line which will join either end of the worm back on itself, thus losing the game.

For example, in the game illustrated below, the player whose turn it is to move is bound to lose since, no matter which end he plays, he has to join the worm back on itself.

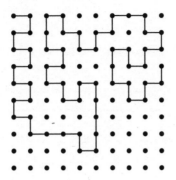

MATCHSTICK GAMES

• • •

Times are changing, but you should still be able to get hold of a box of matches when you are out and about. Many cafés and restaurants like a candle-lit ambience and many waiters and waitresses like occupied kids (and adults) so are willing to lend a box out from behind the bar.

The majority of these games are two-player games along a theme, but a couple are fun to play with larger groups and all are devilishly entertaining.

If your inner Health-and-Safety officer makes you reluctant to encourage anyone to play a game with matches, even spent ones, you can use toothpicks instead. If the sharp points on toothpicks alarm you, too, you can either blunt them or find some paper or plastic drinking straws and cut them into matchstick-length playing pieces.

All Square

Each player has forty matches. Players take it in turn to play and can only play one match at a time. Each match played must touch one end of a match already played at an angle of 90 degrees or 180 degrees:

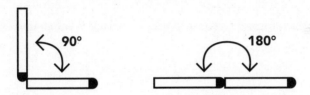

There can be no more than eight matches in any one horizontal or vertical row. The player who plays a match that completes a square scores 1 point for the square and gets an extra turn. When all the matches have been played, the player with most points is the winner.

Columns and Rows

Columns and Rows was invented by Piet Hein, a remarkable Danish mathematician, inventor and poet (among other things) who also invented the board game Hex. It is a two-player game in which, not surprisingly, the matches — and you can have any number you like — must be set out in columns and rows. The columns are vertical lines. The rows are horizontal ones.

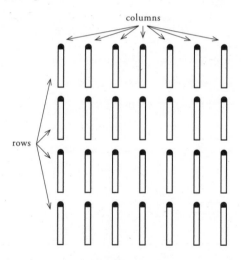

The players take it in turns to move and, on his go, each player can take any number of matches from any one row or any one column, but the matches he takes must be next to each other, with no intervening gaps.

For example, if this is how the table looks after a few moves:

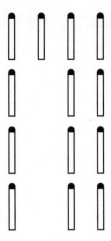

then the next player can take either the whole of the first column,

or the one match in the second column,
or the whole of the third column,
or the whole of the fourth column,
or the whole of the first row,
or the first match or the last two matches in the second row,
or the first match or the last two matches in the third row,
or the first match or the last two matches in the fourth row,
or any single individual match.

What he cannot do is take the whole of the second, third or fourth row, because in each case there's a gap between the first match in the row and the last two.

The winner is the player who picks up the last match.

Garden Path

This is a two-player game. Each player will need about fifteen matches and each player's matches should be clearly distinguishable from those of their opponent. You could use matches with heads of two different colours or else use ink or crayon to colour them. You also need a board, which can be drawn on card or paper. The board consists of a grid of twenty-five squares. The sides of the squares should be just a fraction greater than the length of the matches being used. The sides of the grid should be labelled North, South, East and West.

Each player in turn puts one of their matches on any vacant line on the board. One player's objective is to form a continuous path from North to South, and the other player's objective is to form a continuous path from East to West. Each player, of course, will attempt to block their opponent while at the same time trying to complete their path.

The first player to complete their path is the winner.

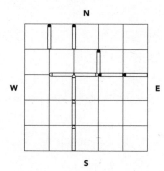

Kayles

'Kayle' is an old word for a skittle, and you could play this game outdoors and with skittles if you had the equipment and the space. It is more usually played indoors, with matchsticks at a table. It is one of several ingenious matchstick games devised by Henry Dudeney, an eminent Victorian and prince among puzzlers. The son of a Sussex schoolmaster and the grandson of a shepherd, Dudeney was a self-taught mathematician who loved puzzles, games and brainteasers above all else – except, perhaps, Mrs Dudeney.

The game calls for two players and as many matches as you like. If you use a thousand, the game will get tedious. If you use five, it will be over in a flash. Twenty is about right. The matches should be laid out on the table so that they are just touching:

— — — — — — — — — — — — — — — — — — — —

When it is her turn, a player can either take one match or she can take two matches, providing those two matches are touching. For example if there were three matches left in the row and it was your turn

1 2 3
— — —

you could either take matches 1 and 2 or you could take matches 2 and 3 or you could just take 1 or 2 or 3. Suppose you chose to take match 2:

$$1 \quad 3$$
$$\underline{\quad} \quad \underline{\quad}$$

Your unfortunate opponent would only be able, in his turn, to take either 1 or 3. He couldn't take both because they are not touching.

In Kayles, the winner is the player who picks up the last match.

Matchboxes

In order to play this game you will need more than one full box of matches as 220 are required.

The matches are laid out in a square grid. Each player in turn may remove one match or he may remove any two matches that are touching (either in a straight line or at right angles). The player who removes the last match is the winner.

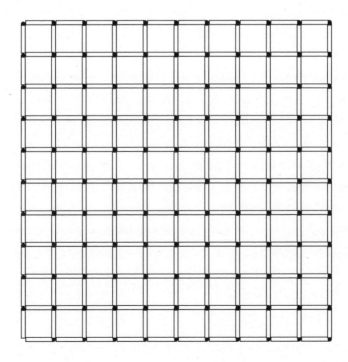

Match-Taker

Like Spillikins (page 152), this game isn't a battle of wits where only two can play; it's more of a light-hearted party piece for the whole family. You can have any number of players and each player must have three matchsticks. As well as the players, you need a leader to play the part of the Match-Taker.

The Match-Taker begins by giving every one of the players a number. If, for example, there are four players, one of them will be Number One, one will be Number Two, and so on. When the players have their numbers, the Match-Taker tells a story. It can be any kind of story about anything he fancies, but into it he will bring the numbers of the different players. Just after he mentions a number he taps the table with his hand. Now, if *he* taps the table before the player whose number has been mentioned manages to tap the table, the Match-Taker takes one of that player's three matches as a penalty. However, if the player whose number was mentioned by the Match-Taker taps the table before the Match-Taker does, the player holds on to his matches. Any player tapping the table by mistake must give up one of his matches to the Match-Taker as well.

The game goes on until all the players have lost their matches to the Match-Taker, at which point it becomes someone else's turn to be the Match-Taker and tell the tale.

Maxey

Τhis game was invented by a marvellous games-mad American called Maxey Brooke. You will need two players, ten matches and a piece of paper and a pencil.

Draw seven parallel vertical lines on the paper – this is your playing area. The lines should be about the same length as a match in height and placed a little less than a match-length apart on the paper.

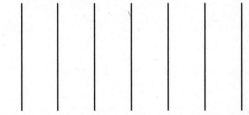

Players start with five matches each, and each player in turn plays one match. A player may place his match on to one of the parallel lines or, if two adjacent lines are occupied by matches, he may 'bridge' those two matches by playing a match across them. Any pair of matches may only be bridged once.

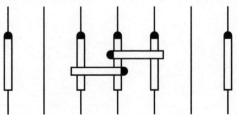

A player scores 1 point each time he plays a match on to a line next to a line that is already occupied by a match, and 2 points each time he forms a bridge between two matches. The player with the most points when all the matches have been played is the winner.

Nim

Nim is the oldest and most famous of all the matchstick games. From its origins in ancient China to new beginnings as one of the first-ever computerised games, via a stint in French new wave cinema, if you haven't discovered it yet you've got a treat in store. It's simple. It's exciting. It's satisfying. In fact, unless you happen to be *very* hard to please, Nim's a game that should keep you totally enthralled from now till your dying day. Here's how it works.

Begin by laying out fifteen matches like this:

  —

  — —

  — — —

  — — —

  — — —

  — —

  —

Seven in the first row, five in the second and three in the third. Each player in turn has to pick up any number of matches from any one of the rows. They may pick up only one match, the whole row, or any number in between – but only from one row at a time. The player who picks up the last match is the winner.

Variation one

The game is played exactly as described above, but the winner is the player who forces their opponent to pick up the last match.

Variation two

The game may start with any number of rows, containing any number of matches. Try it, for example, with five rows containing four, five, six, seven and eight matches.

Gyles says: I was introduced to Nim in 1961, when, aged thirteen, I managed to see Alain Resnais' famous film *L'Année Dernière à Marienbad (Last Year in Marienbad)*. The game features in the film. I made no sense of the movie, none at all, but I understood the game *completely* and have not stopped playing it since.

One-Line Nim

Fifteen matches are laid out in a line.

IIIIIIIIIIIIIII

Each player in turn has to pick up one, two or three matches. The winner is the player who forces their opponent to pick up the last match. You may also try playing One-Line Nim with twenty-one or twenty-five matches instead of fifteen.

Niminy-Piminy

Here's another game from the Nim collection, this time calling for a row of twenty-five matches.

Again, you need two players and each player takes it in turn to pick up one, two or three matches. However, unlike most of the matchstick games, in this game it doesn't matter who picks up the last match. What counts in Niminy-Piminy is the *number of matches you end up with* after all the matches have been picked up. If you end up with an even number of matches, you've won. If you end up with an odd number of matches, you've lost. Bad luck.

To be sure of winning, you've got to see to it that you create one of these two situations: *either* your opponent has an even number of matches in his hand and there are 20, 17, 9 or 4 matches left in the row, *or* he has an odd number of matches in his hand and there are 21, 16, 13, 8 or 5 matches left in the row.

Odd or Even

A ny number of players can get involved in this game. In fact, it's a great getting-to-know-you game, ideal when you want to encourage a group of people to break out of their comfort zones and do a bit of mingling.

You will need ten coins for each player (or matchsticks can be substituted, if you are few days off payday). Each player is armed with their ten coins. Putting any number of them in one of his hands, he holds out his clenched fist to any other player whom he might choose as an opponent and demands 'Odd or even?' The opponent, if she guesses wrongly, receives a coin; if she guesses correctly, she hands over a coin. The two players then reverse roles, the opponent going through the same rigmarole with some of his coins. The two players then split up and seek new opponents.

The first player to succeed in getting rid of all their coins is the winner. (The player who finishes with most coins is the loser, but may be allowed to keep them as a small compensation for their bad luck.)

Spillikins

If Nim and One-Line Nim, Battleships and Aggression, Columns and Rows and Maxey and All Squares have left you exhausted and your brain befuddled, Spillikins is what you need. It isn't a high-powered game like the others. It isn't difficult. It isn't demanding. It's just delicious.

To play Spillikins you need an egg cup (or tea-light holder, or little pot that has the packets of sugar and sweetener in it), a box of matches and two or more players. Stand the matches inside the egg cup and let the players take it in turns to move.

The first player removes one match from the egg cup and carefully lays it across the top of the other matches left in the egg cup. The second player does the same. So does the third. And so it goes on around the group, with players removing the matches from the egg cup one by one and laying them across the top of the remaining matches, until all the matches have been taken out of the egg cup and have been laid across the top, when the game is over.

Of course, a player is going to be very lucky indeed if, in the course of taking a match out of the egg cup and laying it across the top, he doesn't knock over other matches. Every match he knocks over during his moves he must collect and hold in his hand.

At the end of the game, the player with the fewest matches in his hand is the winner.

Take the Last

Place fifty matches in a heap on the table. Each player in turn has to take matches from the heap, and may take any number he pleases between one and six. The player who takes the last match is the winner.

Alternatively the game may be played as follows. Each player has three lives. As before, each player in turn takes up to six matches from the heap. But this time the player who takes the last match loses a life. When a player loses all their lives they drop out of the game. The winner is the last player left when all the others have dropped out.

FIVESTONES

• • •

Fivestones

To play Fivestones you would traditionally use the knucklebones of sheep, but if you don't happen to have any sheep knuckles kicking around, some small pebbles will do nicely instead.

The game consists of a series of lesser games to be played with the stones, in which they are thrown into the air and caught again in various ways. There is an almost infinite variety of these lesser games, and they may be played in any order. The players should agree beforehand the games to be played and the sequence (usually in order of increasing complexity). Each player in turn then goes through the sequence of games until she fails on one of them, and it then becomes the next player's turn. When a player's turn comes round again, she recommences with the game in which she failed on her previous turn. The first player to complete the sequence successfully is the winner. Many of the games start with the same basic throw. The stones are thrown up into the air from the palm of the hand, and as many as possible are caught on the back of the hand. They are thrown from the back of the hand and as many as possible are caught in the palm.

Ones

The player performs the basic throw, as described above. If she succeeds in catching all five, she immediately goes on to the next game. If she catches none, she has failed and the turn passes to the next player.

Otherwise, she transfers all but one of the stones she has caught to her other hand. The single stone is thrown in the air, one of the fallen stones is gathered in the throwing hand, and the thrown stone is caught in the same hand. One of these two stones is transferred to the other hand. This process is repeated until all the stones on the floor have been gathered.

Twos

The five stones are scattered on the ground. One stone is picked up and thrown into the air, two of the stones on the ground are gathered into the throwing hand, and the thrown stone is caught in the same hand. Two stones are transferred to the other hand. The process is repeated, gathering the remaining two stones from the floor.

Threes

This is played in the same way as Twos, except that three stones are gathered on the first throw and the remaining stone on the second throw.

Fours

This is like Twos except that all four stones on the floor must be gathered in one throw.

Pecks

The basic throw is performed, and if all five stones are caught the player immediately goes on to the next game. Otherwise she keeps all the caught stones in her hand, holding one of them between thumb and forefinger. This stone is thrown into the air, one of the stones on the floor is gathered in the throwing hand and the thrown stone is caught in the same hand. This process is repeated until all five stones have been gathered into the throwing hand.

Bushels

The player performs the basic throw. If all five stones are caught she goes on to the next game; if none are caught her turn ends. Otherwise she throws in the air all the stones in her hand, one of the stones on the floor is gathered in the throwing hand, and all the thrown stones are caught in the same hand. This is repeated until all the stones have been gathered in the same hand.

Claws

The game begins with a modification of the basic throw. The player throws the five stones and attempts to catch them on the back of her hand. If none are caught her turn ends. If all five are caught the player attempts to complete the basic throw and if she is successful she goes on to the next game. If one or more, but not all five, are caught on the back of the hand they remain there while the player picks up the remaining stones on the ground between the fingers of her throwing hand – no more than one stone between any two fingers. She then throws the stones from the back of her hand and catches them in her palm. The stones held between the fingers must then be manoeuvred into the palm – without using the other hand.

Ones Under the Arch

The five stones are scattered on the floor. The player forms an arch by touching the thumb and forefinger of the non-throwing hand to the floor.

One stone is picked and thrown into the air. Before it is caught again in the throwing hand one of the remaining stones must be knocked under the arch. This is repeated until all four stones have been knocked under the arch. The arch is then removed, the stone is thrown into the air and the other four stones are gathered into the throwing hand and the thrown stone is caught in the same hand.

Twos Under the Arch

This is the same as Ones Under the Arch except that two stones must be knocked under the arch on each throw.

Threes Under the Arch

Three stones must be knocked under the arch on the first throw, and the remaining stone knocked under the arch on the second throw.

Fours Under the Arch

All four stones must be knocked through the arch at the same time.

Stables

The five stones are scattered on the floor. The fingers and thumb of the non-throwing hand are spread out and placed so that the fingertips are touching the floor and the palm is raised, the spaces between the fingers forming the four stables. One stone is thrown into the air, and before it is caught one of the other stones must be knocked into one of the stables. In this manner a stone is knocked into each of the four stables in turn. The non-throwing hand is then moved away, the throwing hand and the thrown stone is caught in the same hand.

Toad in the Hole

The five stones are scattered on the floor. The non-throwing hand is placed so that the thumb lies straight on the floor with the fingers curled round to form a hole. One stone is thrown into the air and before it is caught again in the throwing hand one of the remaining stones must be picked up and dropped into the hole. This is repeated until all four stones have been dropped into the hole. The non-throwing hand is moved away, the throwing stone is thrown into the air, the four stones are gathered into the throwing hand, and the thrown stone is caught in the same hand.

Snake in the Grass

Four of the stones are placed in a straight line, about six inches (that's 15 cm) apart. The fifth stone is thrown into the air and before it is caught again in the same hand one of the end stones is moved. The moved stone must follow the path shown round the other stones and back to its starting-point.

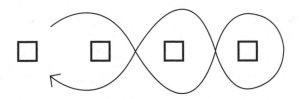

As many throws as required may be taken to complete the manoeuvre, provided that on each throw the end stone is moved part of the way and provided that no other stone is touched.

The RACE is ON

Welcome to our selection of racing games designed to bring out your competitive streak. *These games are great to play at parties because, as a rule, when the race is on it is a case of the more the merrier. One fun way to spend an afternoon is to choose a range of these racing games and have your own mini-tournament. We have put together a suggested selection on page 176, but feel free to devise your own itinerary from a mix and match of all the games on offer. If you are going with the mini-tournament concept, establish teams at the start of proceedings and keep a running score. Add to the fun by choosing team names, mottos and even team colours to wear. Take inspiration from Harry Potter and call yourself Gryffindor, Slytherin and Hufflepuff, or name yourselves after the planets, the street you live in, your favourite animal. Just be sure to cheer for your team as loudly as you can. Play up! Play up! And play the game!*

Gyles says: 'Play up! Play up! And Play the Game!'
That's my motto and it comes, of course, from the famous poem *Vitaï Lampada* ('The Torch of Life') by the eminent Victorian/Edwardian barrister, writer and government adviser, Sir Henry Newbolt (1862–1938). His poetry is somewhat serious stuff, but he was actually rather a fun fellow – and a player in every sense. (He enjoyed a *ménage à trois* with his wife and her girlfriend, who was also his mistress. Oh yes, Henry Newbolt put the racy into racing games.)

Saethryd says: In this book we have been keen to make sure all the games can be played with everyday objects from around the house. Some require slightly less common objects – thimbles, ping-pong balls and the like. Where appropriate, we have suggested alternatives and you should normally be able to find something in the house to act as a substitute, but, as a family, what we have discovered over the years is that it is really useful, and fun, to cultivate a 'games chest'.

Basically, a games chest is just a box where we have collected bits and pieces that come in handy for playing games: old matchboxes – full and empty – lengths of string, ties or socks to act as blindfolds, buttons, ping-pong balls, tennis balls, feathers, old newspapers and magazines, hats, weird and unusual objects for drama/story-telling games, foreign coins, and various other paraphernalia. It always adds to the sense of occasion when we get out the games chest and sometimes just searching through it provides us with the inspiration to come up with a totally new (and bonkers) pastime.

A-Tissue

In order to play this game you will need two pieces of tissue paper and as many straws as there are players. The players, all holding straws in their mouths, divide into teams and each team arranges itself in a circle. The team leaders are then each given a piece of tissue paper, about fifteen centimetres square, which they place on the ends of their straws. To hold the paper there, they must draw breath. They then turn to the next player in the circle and try to pass the paper on to him or her.

The best way to pass the paper from one person to the next is for the player passing it to breathe out just at the moment when the player receiving it breathes in. The paper is passed like this right round the team and back to the leader. The first team to finish has won.

If a piece of paper falls to the ground, the player passing it is allowed to pick it up and put it back on the end of their straw. At no other time may players touch either the tissue paper or the straws.

Balloon Race

This is an ideal game to play at a party because you need balloons, and any party worth its salt will have balloons by the bucket-load. The competitors stand at one end of the room, and each is given a balloon of a different colour. They race to the far end of the room and back again, taking their balloons with them. The only restriction is that the balloons may not be held – they must be moved along by being patted or kicked. Any player who holds their balloon is sent back to the start and has to begin all over again.

Bang Bang Race

In order to play this game you will need some empty paper bags. These are not as common as they once were, so you might want to buy some in advance and play this as a special party game rather than an everyday occurrence. Kids love it because it's noisy and raucous. Adults aren't so keen, for exactly the same reasons.

The players divide into teams and the teams sit facing each other in two rows about two metres apart. Underneath each player's chair is an empty paper bag. On the word 'Go!' the first player in each team gets up, races behind the two teams and back to his own chair. As soon as he sits down, he picks up his paper bag, blows it up and bursts it by hitting it hard with his hand. The bursting of the bag is the signal for the second player to set out round the chairs and back, at which point he blows up his bag and bursts it, and so on down the line.

The first team to have burst all its bags has won.

Biscuit Race

For this game you will need two teams, one umpire and lots of biscuits.

The umpire stands at the end of the room with two chairs on either side of her and a box of dry biscuits, while the teams line up at the opposite end of the room.

'Ready, steady, go!'

The first player in each team races to their chair, they sit down and are given two biscuits, which they have to eat. Then they must whistle clearly, which is not as easy as you might think with a dry mouth full of biscuit crumbs, before getting up and running back down to their teams, at which point the next player races off.

The first team in which everyone has eaten, whistled and run is the winning team and gets a well-deserved drink to wet their whistle.

Blow Ball

For this game you will need some ping-pong balls, which you might not necessarily have kicking around at home. If you don't, it's worth investing in a few: they are cheap as chips and very useful when it comes to creating and playing lots of games. Blow Ball is just one . . .

Here is how you play. Starting at one end of the room, each competitor, on hands and knees and using a drinking straw, has to move a ping-pong ball to the other end of the room and back again by blowing through a straw. Any competitor who touches the ball with the straw or with any part of their body is sent back to the start.

The first player to complete the course successfully is the winner.

Rory says: I love this game.

Gyles says: Notwithstanding the sound of its name and its popularity in China today, the game of ping-pong was invented by the British when the British Empire was at its height. The early rackets were made of pieces of parchment stretched over a small frame and the sound generated in play gave the game its nicknames of 'wiff-waff' and 'ping-pong'. (I told you those years I spent in *Countdown*'s Dictionary Corner weren't wasted!)

Deportment Relay

In the olden days 'gels' of a certain sort were sent to finishing schools where they were taught to be 'young ladies'. Proper posture was a must, and in order to perfect it the girls were made to walk around with books balanced on top of their heads, just so.

This game takes its inspiration from these 'deportment' lessons, but is much more fun. And you *definitely* don't have to be any sort of lady to play it.

Divide the players into two teams. Split the teams so half are at either end of the room. The first players in each team are given a fairly large and heavy book. It is important the books are of comparable weight and size so the race is fair. (We favour the complete works of Shakespeare or a volume of the *Oxford English Dictionary* – naturally.)

When the whistle is blown, the first player in each team sets off across the room balancing the book on their head. They must not touch it with their hands at all until they meet the next member of their relay team at the other end of the room, at which point they pass the book over. The first relay team to complete the race is the winner. If the book falls from a player's head at any point, that player must go back to the start of their portion of the race.

Doll Dressing

This game is fun to play for adults and children alike, but it helps if you have young children as you are far more likely to have some dolls or soft toys at home. Or you may be one of those grown-ups that still sleeps with their teddy bears . . . (No judgement here: we certainly are!)

Players are divided into pairs. Each pair is given an undressed doll or teddy and some clothes to put on it. The winning pair will be the one that manages to dress its doll first, the only problem being that they must only use *one hand each*. It doesn't matter which hand a player chooses to use, but she must keep her other hand firmly behind her back throughout the race.

Gyles says: In the 1980s my wife and I founded the Teddy Bear Museum in Stratford-upon-Avon. When I became an MP in 1992, some at Westminster took a dim view of a parliamentarian whose hobby was collecting teddy bears, but as sex and money scandals began to bring down a number of my colleagues it became clear that a harmless enthusiasm for teddy bears wasn't such a poor choice of pastime after all. And the teddy bear, of course, gets his name from a politician of real achievement and distinction: Theodore 'Teddy' Roosevelt Junior (1858–1919), 26th President of the United States of America.

Drop the Lot

In order to play this game you will need twelve or more empty matchboxes.

The players divide into teams and stand behind their leaders. On the ground in front of each leader are six or more empty matchboxes. On the word 'Go!' the leader picks up the matchboxes, turns around and drops them at the feet of the player behind him, and so on down the line until the last player picks them up and runs to the front of the line, where he drops them at the feet of the new leader, who picks them up once more, turns round and drops them. This goes on till the original leader is the last person in the line and has the matchboxes dropped in front of him. He picks them up, runs back to his original position at the front of the team and shouts 'Finished!' The first team to finish wins.

If six matchboxes seem too easy to handle, try eight!

Head Space

For this great parlour game you will need an even number of players and at least four of them. The players must divide into pairs and each pair counts as one team. Give each team one tennis ball. (Tennis balls are best, but if you haven't got enough, rubber balls or ping-pong balls or even oranges will do.)

Line up the teams along one side of the room and tell them that all they have to do is race to the other side of the room and back again. The first team to get back to the starting-point wins. If that sounds too easy, well it *is* too easy. There's a catch, of course, and, as you've guessed, the catch has got something to do with the tennis balls – or rubber balls or ping-pong balls or oranges.

The two players in each team have got to hold their tennis ball *between their foreheads*. This means that they will have to race along sideways keeping their heads together so that the ball balanced between them doesn't slip away. If the ball *does* slip, two things will happen: the players will bang their foreheads together (which doesn't matter much), and they will have to go back to the starting line and begin all over again (which matters a good deal).

The first team to complete the course with their ball wedged firmly in position wins the race.

Knot Race

Divide the players into two teams and give each team a piece of string, fairly thick if possible and roughly a metre in length depending on the number of players.

The teams line up and the piece of string is given to the first player. On the word 'Go!' the first player ties a knot in the piece of string and passes it on to the second player in the team, who does the same, and so on till the piece of string reaches the last player. When the last player has tied their knot, they race to the front and give the piece of string back to the first player and then return to their position. The first player then has to *untie* one knot and pass it on to the second, who unties another, and so on till it reaches the last player, who unties the last knot.

The winning team is the one that ties and unties all the knots first.

Map Race

This is a game designed to introduce the satnav generation to the joys (and challenges) of map-reading. It is a game for two players (or two small teams of players) and to play it you need two identical maps of the same city. The more detailed the maps, the better the game will be.

All you do is give one map to each player (or team) and on the word 'Go!' give them both the name of a street. The first player to find that street on the map gains a point. After ten rounds, and ten streets, the player/team with most points is the winner.

MINI-TOURNAMENT

• • •

As we mentioned in the introduction to this chapter, a great way to while away a wet Wednesday afternoon or a sunny Sunday morning is to get together and play a whole range of racing games. The next five games make up our five-race programme to get you started.

Ankle Race

The competitors line up at one end of the room, each one crouching or bending down and grasping their ankles. They must race to the other end of the room and back again in this position. Any competitor who takes their hands away from their ankles is sent back to the start.

Back-to-Back Race

The players compete in pairs, each pair standing back-to-back with their arms linked at the elbows. Starting at one end of the room, the linked pairs race to the other end and back again.

Nose Ball

This is the same as Blow Ball (page 169), but now the players have to push the ping-pong balls with their noses.

Piggy-Back Race

The players compete in pairs. One member of each pair climbs on to the other's back to be carried. Starting at one end of the room, the pairs of competitors race to the other end of the room. There the rider dismounts, and he has to carry his partner back to the starting-point.

Three-Legged Race

The players compete in pairs and you will need a scarf for each pair. The players stand side by side, and a scarf is used to tie the right leg of one player to the left leg of the other. Starting at one end of the room, the pairs race to the other end of the room and back again.

Newspaper Race

This is a jolly, lively racing game that is also good to play outside if it is not too windy. The only equipment you will need is an old newspaper.

Before the race begins, each player is armed with two half-sheets of newspaper. They must use these as stepping stones, standing on one while they put the other down in front of them, then moving on to it, picking up the one behind and placing that in front of them, and so on.

The first player to complete the course using their newspaper stepping-stones is the winner. Any player who touches the floor with any part of their body is sent back to the starting-point and has to begin all over again. Anyone stepping off their stepping-stone is disqualified.

Pick and Cup Race

For this game you will need a number of small unbreakable items, such as buttons, apples, pebbles, balls of wool.

Form two teams and get the teams to sit on the floor facing each other, about one metre apart. In each team the first player is a Pick, the next a Cup, the next a Pick, the next a Cup, and so on down the line. Every other player must be a Cup, but the first and last players in each team must be Picks. The Cups hold their hands together in front of them to form a cup and sit as still as bone china.

At the head of each column place at least ten small articles in a neat pile – an apple, an orange, a potato, a button, a book, a ball, a handkerchief, a toy car, a sugar lump and a spoon would do nicely, but be sure that exactly the same items are in both piles.

On the word 'Go!' the player at the head of each team picks up one of the items from the pile and places it in the hands of the Cup. The next Pick then takes it out of the first Cup and places it in the next Cup, and so on, until the last player, who is a Pick, places it on the floor beside him.

As soon as the first player has picked up one item and placed it in the cup next to him, he must pick up the next item and pass it on in the same way. The idea is to get all the items from one end of the line to the other as quickly as possible, so the team with the fastest Picks will win.

Potato Race

For this game you will need three potatoes for each competitor and a cardboard box.

The cardboard box is placed at one end of the room; all the potatoes are placed in a pile at the other end. The players are lined up beside the box. They have to run to the other end of the room, pick up a potato, bring it back and drop it in the box. They repeat this procedure twice more, and the first player to drop three potatoes in the box is the winner.

Saethryd says: Truth be told, you only need potatoes because it's called the Potato Race. If you haven't got any potatoes in the store cupboard, feel free to turn it into the Grapefruit Race, the Apple Race, the Random Cans That Have Been Lingering at the Back of the Store Cupboard for Years Race . . .

Spoon Ball

For Spoon Ball you will need two ping-pong balls and as many spoons as there are players.

The players divide into two teams and each team forms a line. The aim of the race is to pass the ball from spoon to spoon down the line as quickly as possible . . . bearing in mind that the players are holding the spoons in their mouths!

The leader begins by placing a ping-pong ball in his spoon, then turns round and tries to pass the ball to the next in line who is waiting to receive it in the spoon he is holding in his mouth. If the ball is dropped, it can only be picked up by the spoon still held in the mouth. No hands are allowed in this race. The first team to get its ping-pong ball from one end to the other has won.

Thimble Race

This is a good game for a party as, ideally, you need ten or more players. You will also need two thimbles (or a substitute if your sewing kit is looking a little empty . . . we've found a screw-off bottle cap works just as well) and as many straws as there are players.

Divide the players into two teams and get the teams to stand in straight lines. Give each player a straw and give the leader of each team a thimble for her to place on the end of her straw. The straws must at all times be held in the players' mouths and no player must touch either their straw or the thimble with their hands. On the command 'Go!' the leaders must attempt to transfer the thimbles from their straws on to the straws of the players next to them in line, who must in their turn pass them to the players behind them. The first team successfully to have transferred its thimble from the front of the line to the back wins the game. If a thimble falls to the ground at any stage it must be returned to the leader, who starts all over again.

Tortoise Race

This is an unusual race in that the aim is to be the last to finish.

Starting at one end of the room, the competitors 'race' to the other end as slowly as possible. They must go in a straight line towards the other end of the room, and are not allowed to stop. Once the race is on, they must continue moving, however slowly. The last to finish is the winner.

Two-Minute Race

Before the game begins any clocks in the room are removed or covered up, and any wristwatches are confiscated. Starting at one end of the room, the players then 'race' to the opposite wall in exactly two minutes. The competitors can move as slowly as they like, but they must never stop moving, and they have to use their own sense of timing to complete the course when they think two minutes have passed.

The competitors are timed by an umpire who is provided with a watch with a second hand. The winner is the player who is nearest to the wall at the moment when the two minutes have elapsed.

Some sad individuals, either because of a deprived childhood or a mistaken sense of intellectual superiority, tend to deprecate party games. As soon as the genial host appears to be donning his party hat and talking optimistically about Charades, the games-hater looks at her watch and suddenly realises that she promised the babysitter she'd be back before nine. Obviously there is no point in forcing a reluctant guest into a riotous game of Blind Man's Buff, but it is worth coaxing her into something more gentle and, ostensibly, more cerebral. Of course, there is always a case to be made for games that call for mental agility. Let's face it: so much of what we encounter these days — be it TV, magazines, music or even the newspapers — seems to be designed to turn our brains to mush that it's good to be offered a playful mental workout. So sharpen your wits and pencils as we present a plethora of word, number and pencil-and-paper games designed to challenge the mind and enliven the soul. And for the mini-Einsteins amongst us, on page 240 we offer a selection of games specifically for the younger brainbox.

AA

A A has nothing to do with accountants, architects, amateur athletics, automobiles or alcoholics. It is simply a pencil-and-paper challenge that few can resist.

Each player is invited to write down a letter of the alphabet; any letter she likes will do. Now, the host explains that each player must write down a brief anecdote, short story, scenario, biography or verse in which every word begins with the letter the player has put at the top their paper. Ten minutes are allowed, at the end of which the players must read out their efforts and elect a winner.

Acrostics

A word of six or seven letters is chosen, and each player writes the word down in a column on the left-hand side of a sheet of paper. They then write the same word in another column to the right of the first one, but this time with the letters in reverse order. Let us say the chosen word is CARAMEL, then each player's sheet of paper would look something like this:

C	L
A	E
R	M
A	A
M	R
E	A
L	C

The players are then given five minutes in which they have to write the longest word they can think of, beginning and ending with each pair of letters provided by the two columns.

The players score 1 point per letter for each of their words, and the player with the highest total score is the winner. Here's an example:

C	hape	L		= 6
A	ppl	E		= 5
R	hyth	M		= 6
A	lgebr	A		= 7
M	othe	R		= 6
E	xtr	A		= 5
L	ogi	C		= 5
			Total =	40

C	ontractua	L		= 11
A	dministrativ	E		= 14
R	egionalis	M		= 11
A	spidistr	A		= 10
M	usketee	R		= 9
E	uthanasi	A		= 10
L	inguisti	C		= 10
			Total =	75

Alpha

This is a word-listing game in which the players have a time limit of ten minutes in which to list words beginning and ending with the same letter of the alphabet. There are two different versions of the game.

In the first version the players simply have to list as many words as they can that end with the same letter with which they begin. The winner is the player who produces the longest list of such words.

In the second version, which is a more demanding test of vocabulary, each player writes the letter of the alphabet down the left-hand margin of a sheet of paper. Then for each letter they have to find the longest possible word which begins and ends with that letter. When the time limit has expired, the players score 1 point for each letter of each word they have listed and the player with the highest total score is the winner. One player's completed list might look something like this:

A	AMNESIA	= 7
B	BEDAUB	= 6
C	CYCLONIC	= 8
D	DEDICATED	= 9
E	EVERYONE	= 8
F	FLUFF	= 5
G	GRADUATING	= 10
H	HUNCH	= 5

I
J
K   KAYAK   = 5
L   LONGITUDINAL   = 12
M   METAMORPHISM = 12
N   NATIONALISATION = 15
O   OVERDO   = 6
P   PARTNERSHIP   = 11
Q
R   REGULATOR   = 9
S   SUCCINCTNESS   = 12
T   TOURNAMENT   = 9
U
V
W   WINDOW   = 6
X
Y   YELLOWY   = 7
Z

Alphabet Story

Here's a game that will get your creative juices flowing. Allow ten minutes for each player to write down a story of exactly twenty-six words. And each word of the story, which can be punctuated as you please, must start with a successive letter of the alphabet, right the way from A to Z. The most lucid and entertaining story wins the prize.

Anagrams

For this game you will need three or more players, one of whom will be nominated question master. The question master chooses a category such as Countries, Birds, Food, Garden Flowers, Games and Sports, or Rivers, and prepares a list of words belonging to that category. They then prepare another list of the same words, but with the letters of each word jumbled up. The list of jumbled words is placed in a position where all the players can see it, or, alternatively, if you have the time, will and inclination, each player can be given their own copy. A time limit of five or ten minutes is set, in which each player has to discover the principal words by unscrambling the jumbled versions.

The winner is the first player to unscramble all the words correctly or the player with the most correct words when the time limit has expired. Here's an example, using the category Countries:

1. Neaky	5. Nomoac	9. Regalia
2. Rumba	6. Bedraum	10. Agalamute
3. Courade	7. Waliam	11. Englander
4. Wednes	8. Presagion	12. Netsetinchile

The solutions are over the page – but why not test yourself first before turning over!

1. Kenya	5. Monaco	9. Algeria
2. Burma	6. Bermuda	10. Guatemala
3. Ecuador	7. Malawi	11. Greenland
4. Sweden	8. Singapore	12. Liechtenstein

How many did you get?

Arena

The players have ten minutes in which to form as long a list as possible of five-letter words which have a vowel as the first letter, a consonant as the second, a vowel as the third, a consonant as the fourth, and a vowel as the last letter. Such a list might include words such as these:

ARENA	OPERA	UNITE
AROMA	ABODE	AMUSE
ELOPE	AWAKE	OKAPI
EVADE	IMAGE	AGATE

The player who produces the longest list will be the winner.

Big Words

This game is a great time-filler and all you need to play it are two players and some pencils and paper.

Each player is given a list of two-letter combinations, for example EN and RP and UE and FT, and they then have a set period of time in which to write down the longest words that they can think of which contain the two letters in that particular combination. For example, one player might write down ENtry and caRPet and sUE and aFTer, and the other might write down ENtertain and caRPentry and qUEen and craFTy – in which case the second player would have won easily as all his words were longer. It's very simple: the player with the longest words wins.

To get you going, here are some two-letter combinations to try.

AE (aeroplane)
UB (rhubarb)
RC (architect)
MB (combination)
LL (umbrella)
OS (position)
ST (constable)
EC (recitation)
ND (dandelion)
UP (porcupine)

UC (cucumber)
EP (elephant)
AK (pancakes)
TR (orchestra)

Botticelli

Why this game should be named after a fifteenth-century Florentine painter is a moot point. Perhaps it is called 'Botticelli' because people could not agree on the correct pronunciation for 'Breughel'. Whatever its origin, Botticelli is a fascinating guessing game, requiring a fairly good standard of general knowledge.

One player thinks of the name of a famous person or fictitious character – one who should be known to the other players – and tells the other players the initial letter of his subject's surname.

The other players now have to identify the mystery person, and they do this by asking two types of question: direct and indirect. They can only ask *direct* questions if the player has failed to provide a satisfactory answer to an *indirect* question.

For example, if a player chooses to be the great Florentine painter Sandro Botticelli, he will begin the game by saying 'I am someone beginning with a B', and the other players will then ask him a whole series of indirect questions, such as 'Are you a German composer?' or 'Are you a film star?' or 'Are you one of the Spice Girls?' The player must reply 'No, I'm not Bach' or 'No, I'm not Drew Barrymore' or 'No, I am not Mel B, aka Scary Spice'.

However, if he cannot think of an appropriate answer, either because he cannot think of the name of a German composer beginning with B or because his mind has gone blank, the questioner can then put a direct question ('Are you a fact?' 'Are you alive?' 'Are you British?' 'Are you a woman?'), to which a truthful 'Yes' or 'No' answer *must* be given.

Because direct questions require honest answers, it is important that a player chooses a character about which he knows something so as to be able to answer the direct questions properly.

Obviously the players asking the questions will do their best to ask awkward indirect questions so as to get as many opportunities as possible to ask direct questions. When a player asks an indirect question, he must always have an answer to it himself. (For example, he cannot ask 'Were you the captain of HMS *Bounty*?' or 'Are you the King of Celesteville?' if he has not already heard of William Bligh or Babar the Elephant. But who hasn't?)

The questioner can discover the identity of the secret subject in one of two ways: either by asking an indirect question that is so specific that the player has no alternative but to reveal himself ('Are you a Renaissance painter who lived from 1447 to 1510?' 'Yes, I am Botticelli'); or by asking a direct question to which the only answer is the truth ('Are you Botticelli?' 'Yes').

The player who puts the question that reveals the chosen character wins the game and, in the next round, it becomes his turn to choose a character.

Gyles says: Of all the games in the book, this is my favourite. The challenge is to choose a character that everyone playing will definitely know, but who is a far from obvious subject. If you start with a Z, it does not take long to reach Zeus, but P for Harry Potter, Beatrix Potter, Peter Phillips, Peter Pan, Pirandello, Piranesi, Popeye or Ptolemy is pretty much perfection. To avoid arguments, steer clear of characters where the initial of their name may lead to confusion – for example Joan of Arc, Arthur Conan Doyle and HRH Prince William, Duke of Cambridge.

Bulls and Cows

For this game you will need two players, a piece of paper, a pencil and the mind of a mathematical wizard.

Bulls and Cows is a game of logical deduction that is similar to Word Power (page 236), except that numbers not words are to be guessed and the scoring of guesses is rather different. Here's how it's played.

The first player thinks of a four-digit number, for example 4711 or 9362. The second player guesses by proposing any four-digit number. Player one tells player two how close their guess is by saying how many 'bulls' and 'cows' have been scored: a bull means the guess contains a correct digit in the correct position; a cow means that the guess contains a correct digit but in the wrong position. The second player continues guessing until they have enough information to identify the mystery number.

Get it? Got it? Good. We told you these games would test the brain cells. Time for an example, wethinks. Let's say the number thought of by player one was 9362, then the guess and responses might proceed like this.

1234 2 cows (that means that two of the numbers are right but they are not in the right place)

2468 1 bull, 1 cow (one of the numbers is right, and another is right *and* in the correct spot)

1580 nothing

2436 1 bull, 2 cows (getting closer, three are right and one of those is
      in the correct spot)

4367 2 bulls

9362 4 bulls. That's it!

Of course, doing all that guessing and working out in your head would be a stretch even for Pythagoras, which is why it helps to have pencil and paper to hand. That way player two can record their guesses and their scores and work out which digits can be eliminated and what possibilities and combinations remain.

When the mystery number has been guessed, the players change roles and player one has to guess a number thought of by player two. The player who requires the fewer number of guesses to identify the mystery number is the winner.

Categories

To play this old party favourite, give all the players a pencil and some paper and the same long list of different categories. The categories can be as varied as you like. Here are some suggestions to get you started.

AUTHORS

CHEMICALS

ATHLETES

FISHES

FLOWERS

BALLET DANCERS

LAKES

POLITICIANS

TAKE THAT SINGLES

FLUIDS

MAKES OF CAR

CATHEDRAL CITIES

PERFUMES

SEX SYMBOLS

OLYMPIC ATHLETES

SCULPTORS

SCHOOLS

TREES
AIRLINES
STATES OF AMERICA
FILMS
NOBEL PRIZE WINNERS
X FACTOR WINNERS

A letter of the alphabet is then chosen at random and the players have ten minutes in which to think of as many names as possible, beginning with the chosen letter, to go by each category. When the time is up a player is given two marks for every name listed provided it has been listed by *no* other player. If it has been, then each player gets one mark. The player with the most marks is the winner.

For subsequent rounds a new initial letter is chosen. The same categories may be used again or a new list of categories may be selected.

Changelings

This was one of the most popular of all Victorian games and a favourite pastime of that remarkable don and dodo-fancier Lewis Carroll. To play the game you must transform one word into another, changing one letter at a time and creating a new word at every stage.

To play the game competitively, you can turn it into a race with the first player to complete each transformation earning the points. Here are a few examples.

In three steps turn DOG into CAT. (DOG / COG / COT / CAT)

In four steps turn BOY into MAN. (BOY / TOY / TON / TAN / MAN)

In six steps turn SHIP into BOAT. (SHIP / SLIP / SLAP / SLAT / SEAT / BEAT / BOAT)

And (this was Lewis Carroll's favourite) in eight steps turn BLACK into WHITE. (BLACK / SLACK / SHACK / SHARK / SHARE / SHIRE / SHINE / WHINE / WHITE)

Clue Words

This is a game for which pencil and paper are helpful but not essential. They are useful if you want to make notes, which you almost certainly will unless you are very quick witted.

One player begins by thinking of an eight-letter word. The other player now has to guess what it is. To help him guess, the first player will give the second player three clues.

Clue 1 is a three-letter word in which each of the three letters also appears in the mystery eight-letter word. If the second player guesses the word after Clue 1, he scores 3 points.

Clue 2 is a four-letter word in which each of the four letters also appears in the mystery word. If the second player guesses it after Clue 2, he scores 2 points.

Clue 3 is a five-letter word in which each of the five letters also appears in the mystery word. If the second player guesses it after Clue 3, he scores only 1 point.

Supposing the mystery word was MUSHROOM, the first clue might be HUM, which could lead the second player who is guessing to suggest HUMILITY. The second clue might be HUMS, which could lead to

SUBHUMAN being the guess. If the third clue was MUSH, the player would probably guess MUSHROOM at last and score 1 point. If he fails to guess it after he has been given three clues, he gets no points at all. A failed guess means that it is the opponent's turn again, and he chooses another eight-letter mystery word. When a player successfully guesses the mystery word after one, two or three clues, it is then his turn to choose the next mystery word.

After a set number of rounds the player with the highest score is the winner.

Crambo

Crambo, although it is a very unsophisticated game, has been popular for several centuries. Here at Brandreth Towers we are much bigger fans of Dumb Crambo (page 326), but each to their own. Dumb Crambo is the more dramatic version of the game, which is (a) probably why we like it, and (b) why you will find it in the Music and Drama chapter of this book.

With regular Crambo, one of the players thinks of a word and then announces to the other players a word that rhymes with the word he has chosen. For example, he might think of the word 'dull' and announce the word 'hull'. The other players are then each allowed three guesses to discover the word thought of by the first player. If a player guesses the word correctly, he has the honour of choosing the word for the next round. If none of the others guess the word, or if they have all fallen asleep, then the original player has another turn.

Saethryd says: Can you tell we're Dumb Crambo fans? Seriously, go to page 326 – quick, hurry, don't be put off by the whole 'dumb' thing, you won't be compromising your intellectual kudos I promise; there are quotes there from Pepys and everything. Go on, off you go. Trust me, I went to Oxford . . . once, to see that college where they filmed *Harry Potter*.

Crossword

Before the game begins a square grid is drawn with nine squares across and nine squares down. A larger grid may be drawn if a longer game is required. The first player writes a word anywhere in the grid, either across or down, and scores 1 point for each letter in the word. The players then play alternately, each player forming another word which must interlock with one or more of the previously entered letters in crossword fashion, and scoring 1 point for each new letter written. For example, if a player writes the word CROSSWORD, linking the C and W of previously completed words, he would score 7 points – he cannot claim for the C and W. Proper nouns, abbreviations and foreign words are not allowed.

Play continues until neither player can find further letters that can be inserted to form new words. The player with the highest score is the winner.

D	I	S	C	U	S	S		P		Mary	Michael
I			H		T			O			
S	T	R	E	N	U	O	U	S		9	8
T			C		M			T		8	8
U	S		K		B	O	O	M		6	4
R	O	O	M		L			A		2	4
B			A		I		A	N		2	2
E			S	T	O	N	E	D		1	1
D	O		E		G		O	X		1	
										29	27

Crosswords

Although this and the previous game have similar names, they are in fact quite different. (An interesting, though irrelevant, point to note is that the completed grid in the previous game resembles the type of crossword that is popular in Britain, whereas the completed grid in this game resembles the type of crossword that is more popular in France.)

Before the game begins each player draws on their sheet of paper a grid with five squares across and five squares down. If a longer game is required or if there are more than five players, then a larger grid may be used. Each player in turn calls out any letter of their choice. All the players must then enter that letter in their own grids, in any position they choose. Once a letter has been entered, it may not be moved. The aim is to form words either across or down.

The game ends when all the squares have been filled. The scores are worked out according to the number of letters in the words each player has formed. One point is scored for each letter contained in a valid word – one-letter words, proper nouns, foreign words and abbreviations do not count. A letter may not be shared by two or more words in the same row or columns. (Thus if a player has a row that reads CONET the most he can score is 4 points for CONE – he cannot also score points for ON, ONE or NET.) One bonus point is scored for each word that completely fills a row or column.

The player with the highest score is the winner.

Player 1   **Player 2**

D	O	G	M	I	3
A	T	B	E	T	5
R	O	L	I	S	2
T	O	U	G	H	6
F	X	T	O	E	3

4 3 0 4 5

F	O	E	A	T	5
O	R	X	G	M	2
O	B	I	T	H	3
D	O	T	L	I	3
G	U	E	S	T	6

4 3 4 0 3

Score: 35 points   **Score: 33 points**

Donkey

This is a spelling game for two or more players in which the players must build words but never finish them. In order to play you don't need anything about you but your wits, and perhaps a dictionary to resolve any contentious spelling debates.

Let's start with an example. If Adam and Eve were playing . . .

Adam might begin with an A (for 'apple');

Eve might add a C (for 'actor');

Adam could follow that with a T (ending a three-letter word doesn't count);

Eve might continue with an 'I' (thinking now of 'actinal', which would end on Adam);

Adam could counter with an O;

leaving Eve with no alternative but to say N, making 'action', therefore ending a word and losing one of her six lives.

Players cannot pick letters at random. They must be thinking of a specific word, and if their opponents don't believe they are spelling a real word, they can challenge them. If the house dictionary upholds the word, the challenger loses a life. If the word does not appear to have occurred to the compilers of the dictionary, the challenged individual loses a life. Each time you lose a life, you gain a letter. So the first time you become a D, the second time a DO, the third time a DON etc.

The last person to become a donkey – and donkeys are players who have lost all six lives – is the winner.

Gyles says: For what it is worth, and for whoever can manage to remember it, the longest word in the English language is *floccinaucinihililpilification*, meaning (somewhat significantly) 'the action of estimating as worthless'.

Gyles also says: For those unsure of *actinal* it means 'pertaining to that part or surface of a radiate animal which contains the mouth and surrounding organs'.

Guggenheim

There are some people who feel that Guggenheim isn't quite as exciting a game as its unusual name might lead you to expect. There are others (and they are in the majority) who feel that no party is complete without a round or two of this simple but diverting pencil-and-paper entertainment.

Guggenheim is basically a variation of Categories (page 208) and the points scoring system is the same. A list of categories is chosen and each player writes the list down the left-hand margin of their sheet of paper. A key word of five or more letters is then chosen and each player writes the keyword, spaced out, along the top of their sheet of paper. A time limit of ten or fifteen minutes is agreed, and each player must then write down one word beginning with each letter of the keyword for each category.

For example, with a keyword of MAYBE a completed list might look something like this:

	M	A	Y	B	E
Colours	Mauve	Amber	Yellow	Bistre	Ebony
Items of clothing	Mitten	Apron	Yashmak	Blouse	?
Birds	Mallard	Albatross	?	Bantam	Egret
Indoor games	?	Aggression	Yacht	Backgammon	Euchre
Countries	Malaysia	Andorra	Yemen	Burundi	Ethiopia
Poets	Milton	Arnold	Yeats	Burns	Eliot

When the time is up, a player is given 2 points for every word they have listed provided it has been listed by *no* other player – hence the brilliance of offering the unlikely 'bistre' instead of the obvious 'blue'. For words listed by more than one player, only 1 point is given. The player with the most points is the winner.

Hidden Words

To play Hidden Words all you have to do is think of a suitably long word like

ABANDONMENT or BEAUTIFUL or CONTRABAND or DUNDERHEAD or EVERGREEN or FRATERNITY or GEOGRAPHY or HOSPITALITY or IGNORANCE or JOVIALITY or KINGDOM or LONELINESS or METAMORPHOSIS or NATIVITY or OPPORTUNITY or PATRONAGE or QUICKNESS or ROTUNDITY or SERENDIPITY or TANTAMOUNT or UNDERSTANDING or VARICOSE or WEARISOME or XYLOPHONE or ZOOLOGY

(to give you a choice of twenty-six), and make a list of all the words you can think of that can be formed out of the letters contained in the long word. Out of ABANDONMENT alone it is possible to create over forty other words. Choose the word, set a time limit and when the time's up the player with the longest list wins.

Some people are sticklers for rules, and if you are one of those, then here are some common ones often used when playing Hidden Words:

Rule 1: Each word must contain at least four letters.
Rule 2: Proper nouns (names of people, places, etc.) are not allowed.

Rule 3: Foreign words, abbreviations and plurals are not allowed.

Rule 4: A letter may be used in any word no more than the number of times it occurs in the starter word.

It might be a good idea to have a dictionary available to check disputed words. As an example, the following list shows some of the words that might be made from CONTRABAND.

Band	Crab	Cord	Carton	Brand
Bard	Drab	Cobra	Brat	Bacon
Dart	Drat	Cart	Adorn	Road
Baron	Acorn	Card	Abandon	Broad
Barn	Corn	Cant	Trod	Toad

Leading Lights

The name of a well-known person is proposed. Each player has to think of an appropriate phrase which begins with the same initials as the name in question. For example, Wolfgang Amadeus Mozart might prompt the phrases 'Was Austrian Musician' or 'Wrote Appealing Melodies'; Sigmund Freud might give rise to 'Subconscious Fantasies' or 'Sychic Fenomena' (perhaps not) or 'Sex Fiend' (definitely not); Simon Cowell might make players think of 'Someone Charming', and so forth . . .

Little Words

This game is reverse of Big Words, which was explained earlier in this section (page 202). All the players are given a list of pairs of letters, and all they have to do is use each pair of letters in a word. The player who has the list of *shortest* words is the winner.

So if the list was

ND
RT
OP
AG
IP
AT
SK
PE
YO
ZO

and two players came up with the following lists

GRAND	END
PORT	ART
OPEN	TOP

BAG	AGE
SLIP	TIP
HAT	RAT
ASK	SKY
PEAR	PEN
YOU	YOLK
ZONE	ZOO

then the player whose list is on the right is the winner.

Proverbs

It says in the Book of Proverbs that 'A merry heart maketh a cheerful countenance'. And this game has been the cause of many happy hearts and faces since people began playing it back in Victorian times.

If more than two are playing, one player leaves the room while the others decide on a proverb. When the player returns they have to guess the proverb chosen by the other players. This is done by asking each player in turn a question, which may be about any subject under the sun. The first answer must contain the first word of the proverb, the second answer must contain the second word, and so on. When all the words of the proverb have been used, the players begin again with the first word.

For example, if the chosen proverb is 'Look before you leap', the dialogue might proceed as follows:

Question: How old are you?
Answer: I'm older than I *look*, but not as old as I feel.
Question: What is your favourite colour?
Answer: White was my favourite colour *before* I married, but I'm not so sure now.
Question: What time is it?
Answer: It's time *you* bought yourself a watch.
Question: What do you think of the Government?

Answer: I think that their forward-looking policies are a great *leap* backwards.

Question: Where are you going on holiday next year?

Answer: I don't know until I've had a chance to *look* through the brochures.

The questioner is allowed to ask as many questions as he wishes within a time limit of, say, five minutes. An incorrect guess or failure to find the proverb within the time limit means that the questioner must take another turn, otherwise the player who answered the last question becomes the next questioner.

To avoid making the answers too obvious, is it necessary to choose proverbs without awkward words. For example, if the proverb chosen were 'A rolling stone gathers no moss', it might be difficult to contrive an answer in which the word 'moss' didn't stick out like a sore thumb. This problem may be overcome to some extent by making the answers fairly inconsequential (but not too long-winded as this rather spoils the fun) and by attempting to include in the answers plenty of red herrings, such as 'cloud', 'lining', eggs', 'basket', and so on.

Gyles warns: When I first played this game it was at breakfast at an Oxford College. The proverb chosen was an old favourite: 'A nod's as good as a wink to a blind horse'. Unfortunately for me, the clever-clogs of Oxford chose to bamboozle me with a more elaborate version of the same thing: 'A slight inclination of the cranium is as adequate as a spasmodic movement of one optic to an equine quadruped utterly devoid of visionary capacity'.

Rhyme in Time

The essence of this game is that all the players must converse . . . in verse.

Each player takes it in turn to speak a short phrase and the player who follows must come up with a phrase that rhymes with the last one. A player who hesitates or comes up with a phrase that doesn't rhyme drops out. The last player left talking wins the game.

At the beginning of each round a new player should be chosen to start, as the initial player had an obvious advantage.

Gyles says: Any player who ends his first phrase with the word 'orange' is automatically disqualified. There is no known rhyme for 'orange' in the English language. (And it's pretty difficult to find a rhyme for 'silver', too.)

Scaffold

The players are all given the same three letters – R, D, T, for example – and have ten minutes in which to form a list of words which contains those three letters in the order given. Such a list might contain the following if R, D and T were the letters given:

CORDITE	PRODUCT
CORDIALITY	CREDIT
RADIOLOGIST	ARIDITY
RADIATOR	GRADUATE
PREDATOR	INTRODUCTION

Players score 1 point for each word listed, and the player with the highest score is the winner.

Saethryd says: The three letters should be chosen carefully so that it is possible to find a good number of words which use them. Thus L, M, E or R, F, N or M, I, T, for example, would be satisfactory, but Z, Q, N or W, X, F could just possibly result in scores of zero all round (unless you are playing with a group of Serbian lexicographers).

Short Story

A time limit of five or ten minutes is set. Within that time limit each player has to compose a short story. The only restriction is that no word used may contain more than three letters. When the time limit has expired all the stories are read out. The player whose composition is judged to be the cleverest or most amusing is the winner.

Gyles says: Here is my attempt from the last time we played. A valiant effort I thought but, alas, I was not crowned the victor. Well, there's no accounting for taste . . .

A man had a pig in a sty. It ate all he fed it. But one day the pig bit the man. By gum, was the man mad! Now the pig is ham in a can.

Stairway

A letter is chosen and the players are then given ten minutes in which to write down as long a list of words as possible beginning with the chosen letter.

Sounds easy? Here's the twist: the first word of the list must be a two-letter word, the second word a three-letter word, the third a four-letter word, the fourth a five-letter word, and so on. For example:

M
ME
MAN
MINT
MELON
MEADOW
MISSION
MATERNAL
MORTALITY
MISFORTUNE
MAGNIFICENT
MATHEMATICAL
MISCELLANEOUS
MULTIPLICATION
MISAPPREHENSION

At the end of the set period the player with the most impressive stairway – that is, the longest list of words – is the winner.

Stepping Stones

Stepping Stones is a mentally stimulating game of word associations, which may be played on any level from the banal to the esoteric. Each player in turn is given five themes by the other players. For example, a player may be told to get from Music to Astronomy via Cookery, Finance and Cars. He may use up to nine statements or phrases as stepping stones and must touch on each of the themes in the order given. The other players, acting collectively as umpires, must satisfy themselves that all the themes have been touched upon, that the sequence of associations is valid, and that any puns, jokes, allusions and the like are not too far-fetched.

Here are two ways in which the example quoted might work out:

1. Dame Nellie Melba was an opera singer. (Music)
2. Peach Melba was named in her honour. (Cookery)
3. Every peach contains a stone.
4. A stone is fourteen pounds.
5. Pounds are Sterling. (Finance)
6. Stirling Moss was a British racing driver. (Cars)
7. Moss, so they say, is not gathered by rolling stones.
8. The Rolling Stones are rock stars.
9. Stars, in fact, are formed from gas, not from rock. (Astronomy)

1. Musicians usually begin by learning scales. (Music)
2. Scales are found on fish.
3. Salmon is the fish most often served with salads. (Cookery)
4. Salmon may be caught from riverbanks.
5. Banks are financial institutions. (Finance)
6. Bank managers usually play golf.
7. The Golf is an imported car, unlike the Mini. (Cars)
8. Mini Driver is a film star.
9. Stars and planets are what are studied in . . . (Astronomy)

Taboo

For this game you will need at least two players and an umpire.

The umpire chooses any commonly used word – such as 'yes', 'no', 'and', 'is', 'you', 'the' – and declares that word to be taboo. He then asks questions of each of the other players in turn, and each player must reply immediately with a sensible and relevant answer. If the player hesitates, or uses the forbidden word, he is out. The last player to stay in the game is the winner and becomes the umpire for the next round.

In a somewhat more taxing version of this game the umpire declares a certain letter of the alphabet to be taboo and the players must then reply with a sentence that does not contain the forbidden letter.

Telegrams

Each player in turn calls out a letter of the alphabet at random, and all the players write down the letters as they are called out. A list of about fifteen letters should be formed in this way. The players then have five minutes in which each of them has to compose a telegram, the words of which must begin with the listed letters in the order given. Stops (full stops) may be inserted where required and the last word of the telegram may, if the player so desires, be the name of the imaginary sender. For example, if the letters called out were

H, A, I, B, B, A, U, T, L, D, H, S, A, O, C

one player might write:

HAVE ARRIVED IN BLACKPOOL BUT AM UNABLE TO
LOCATE DECK CHAIRS HENCE SAND ALL OVER CYNTHIA

Whereas another player might write:

HURRY AND IMMEDIATELY BRING BACK ALL UNUSED
TEA LEAVES STOP DADDY HATES SUPPING ALE OR COCOA

When the five minutes are up each player reads out their telegram and the winner is the player whose telegram is judged to be the most sensible, the cleverest, the wittiest or the silliest.

Word Power

This is the linguistic version of Bulls and Cows (page 206).

The first player thinks of a five-letter word which has to be guessed by the second player. Guessing the mystery word involves logical deduction and a process of elimination.

The second player proposes any five-letter word and the first player indicates how close this word is to the mystery word by awarding points: 1 point for each letter in the proposed word that corresponds with a letter in the mystery word. Note that the second player is not told which letters are correct, only how many. The second player carries on making guesses until she has enough information to identify the mystery word. You will need pencil and paper for the second player to record her guesses, the points they scored and the letters that can be eliminated.

The players then change roles for the second round, and the first player has to guess a five-letter word thought of by the second player. The winner of the game is the player who identifies the mystery word in the fewest number of guess.

Here is a sample round showing the sort of reasoning required:

1. DANCE   1 point
2. SANDY   2 points
3. HANDY   1 point (there must be an S and no H)
4. SOUND   1 point (that eliminates O, U, N, D which means from guess 2 there must be an A or a Y)

5. SUNNY   1 point (that eliminates Y. The word contains S, A, which means from guess 1 that eliminates C and E)

6. FAILS   2 points (that eliminates F, I, L as we already know that the word contains S and A)

7. STRAP   4 points (the word contains two of the letters from T, R, P)

8. GRASP   3 points (so, the word contains T and no G, and we now have S, A, T plus either R or P and one other or a repeated letter)

9. STAMP   3 points (so it's S, T, A, R and another – no M or P)

10. STRAW   That's it!

A̲ B C̶ D̶ E̶ F̶ G̶ H̶ I̶ J K L̶ M̶ N̶ O̶ P̶ Q R̲ S̲ T̲ U̶ V W̲ X Y̶ Z

Vowels

This is another word-listing game which is a good test of vocabulary. A particular vowel is chosen, and the players have ten minutes in which to produce a list of words which must conform to the following simple rules:

Rule 1: Each word must contain at least five letters.

Rule 2: Each word must contain the chosen vowel twice or more, and must contain no other vowel.

Rule 3: Proper nouns, foreign words and hyphenated words are not allowed.

Here are typical words which might be listed for each chosen vowel:

A CATAMARAN, KAYAK, BALLAD, ANAGRAM, SALAD, BANTAM

E REBEL, PRECEDE, REDEEMER, REFEREE, BEETLE, FEEBLE

I MINIM, CIVIL, PIPPIN, RIPPING, ILLICIT, IMPLICIT

O ROBOT, MORON, COMMON, DOCTOR, CORDON, MONSOON

U   SUBURB, HUMDRUM, UPTURN, SUNBURN, RUMPUS,
    SUCCUBUS

Players score 1 point each time the chosen vowel occurs in each of their words. The player with the highest total score is the winner.

MINI-EINSTEIN

• • •

Now, not for a moment are we suggesting that your little ones are not up to a strenuous game of Bulls and Cows or a competitive round of Changelings, but from little acorns grow mighty oak trees and from simple challenges grow life-long passions for wordplay. Sometimes it's best to run before you can walk, so here are some simple spelling games for the kids (and adults who feel like something a little less taxing on the old brain cells). We've also included some numerical brainteasers. Children love using them to show off to their mates: they are almost like magic tricks and showcase the marvellous mystery that is mathematics. Behold! Our mini-selection for our mini-Einsteins . . .

Spelling Bee

When we are playing this game we like to pretend we are in one of those real Spelling Bees they hold in America where everything is taken VERY seriously . . . as it should be!

One player acts as question-master and calls out a word to each of the other players in turn, who must then give the correct spelling of the word. If the player spells the word correctly a score of 1 point is awarded.

The question-master may call the words from a prepared list or may make up the list as she goes along. It is, of course, most important that the words used should be matched to the abilities of the players taking part. It would be silly to ask a group of six-year-olds to spell words like 'parallel', 'psychological', 'committee' and 'furlough' as it would be to ask an average group of teenagers or adults to spell words like 'door', 'school', 'yellow' and 'horse'.

When a predetermined number of rounds have been played, the player with the most points is the winner.

Variation 1

The game is played as described above, except that a player who fails to spell a word correctly drops out of the game. The winner is the last player left in.

Variation 2

A player who spells a word correctly is given another word to spell. If he spells that correctly, he is given another, and so on. He scores a point for each correct spelling and his turn ends only when he fails to spell a word correctly. The player with the most points at the end of the game is the winner.

Variation 3

The players are divided into two teams sitting opposite each other. The question-master calls out a word to each player in turn, selecting the two teams alternately. A player who spells a word correctly scores a point for their team. If a player fails to spell a word correctly, the same word is offered to their opposite number in the other team, who, if they can spell the word correctly, may score a bonus point for their team.

Backward Spelling

This is a form of Spelling Bee which is made a little more difficult for the players since the words called out have to be spelled backwards. The game may be played in any of the ways described for Spelling Bee.

Vowels Out

The leader gives each player in turn an equally long and equally difficult word to spell. All the player has to do is spell the word correctly, remembering, however, that they must not utter any of the five vowels. When they get to a vowel they must adopt a special sign language: to indicate an A you raise your right arm, to indicate an E you raise your left arm, to indicate an I you point to your own eye, to indicate an O you point to your mouth, and to indicate a U you point to the leader. Any player spelling a word incorrectly, uttering a vowel or mixing up signals drops out. The last player left standing is the winner.

Rory says: I love this game.

The Numbers Game

I n fact, this is not so much a game as a collection of number tricks, phenomena and challenges: mathematical marvels to amaze and amuse you. Memorise them if you can and then use them to amuse and amaze your friends.

All the Ones

$$1 \times 9 + 2 = 11$$
$$12 \times 9 + 3 = 111$$
$$123 \times 9 + 4 = 1111$$
$$1234 \times 9 + 5 = 11111$$
$$12345 \times 9 + 6 = 111111$$
$$123456 \times 9 + 7 = 1111111$$
$$1234567 \times 9 + 8 = 11111111$$
$$12345678 \times 9 + 9 = 111111111$$

Amazing, isn't it?

Amazing Game

If you want your friends to look at you wide-eyed with admiration, try this amazing game on them. Get them all to sit in a circle with pencils and paper. Then tell them to follow your instructions carefully and say:

Write down any five-digit number you like.

Now multiply it by 2.

Now add 5.

Now multiply the result by 50.

Now add your age to the total.

Now add the number of days in the year, 365.

Now subtract 615.

And you will find you're left with a seven-digit number, the first five digits representing the number you first wrote down and the last two digits showing your age. Amazing, isn't it?

Just to prove it really does work, here's an example:

Write down a five-digit number, say	12345
Multiply it by 2, making	24690
Add 5, making	24695
Multiply the result by 50, making	1234750
Add your age, 16, say, making	1234766
Add the number of days in a year, making	1235131
Subtract 615, making	1234516

Amazing Multiplication

Take any three-digit number you like and multiply it by 11. Whatever answer you get, multiply it by 91. The final answer will *always* be the original number written twice; so 123 will become 123123, 857 will become 857857, 999 will be 999999. Incredible but true!

Go on, try it if you don't believe us.

How Old Are You?

You will never need to ask anyone how old they are again if you can persuade them to do a little sum for you and tell you the answer. Give the friend whose age you want to discover a piece of paper and a pencil, and without letting you see what they are writing, get them to do as you instruct.

Write down your age.
Double it.
Add 1.
Multiply the result by 5.
Add 5.
Multiply the result by 10.
Subtract 100.
Cross off the last two digits.
And give me the number you are left with.

Whatever figure your friend gives you will be their age! It seems amazing, but it does work, as you can see in this example:

Sarah writes down her age, which is	13
She doubles it, making	26
She adds 1, getting	27
She multiplies the result by 5, making	135
She adds 5, getting	140
She multiplies the result by 10, making	1400
She subtracts 100, getting	1300

She crosses off the last two digits, leaving   13

And 13, of course, is Sarah's age.

Mind-Reader

Here's a game that will dumbfound your friends and turn you into one of world's great mind-readers. Invite one of your friends to write down on a piece of paper any five-digit number that doesn't end in either a 0 or 1. Get your friend to show you and everyone else the number he's written and now announce a number that is to be the sum of this number and of four others, of which your friend will supply two and you will supply two, all the numbers being five digits.

Now get your friend to write a second number under his first. Now you write a third number under the second number. Now he writes a fourth number under the third number and you write a fifth number under the fourth number. Finally you invite him to add up the five numbers and the grand total will be the exact figure you predicted . . . of course!

The secret of how you manage your mind-reading is simple. When your friend writes down his first five-digit number, you put a 2 in front of it, subtract 2 from its last digit and give the result as your prediction for the final grand total. (So if he writes 68555, you predict that 268553 will be the sum total.)

When you come to add your two five-digit numbers to the sum, you get your numbers by subtracting each of the five digits in his two numbers from 9. So if he writes 22222 under his original number, you simply write 77777 under 22222.

Here's a quick example to make it crystal clear.

Your friend's original number is 12345.
Your prediction for the final number will be 212343.
Write this on a folded piece of paper and give it to someone else to hold for dramatic effect.
Now the sum:

Your friend's original number	12345
He then writes his second number	51515
You now write a number	48484
He then writes another number	17639
You now write a number	82360
He adds all the numbers up	212343

Get your friend to pass you the piece of paper and reveal your mind-bending mind-reading talents.

Rory says: I love this trick. It takes a couple of practices but once you've learnt it your friends really will believe you can read minds!

Trick Multiplication
Here's a trick question that almost certainly won't fool you – because you are clever and quick-witted – but will almost certainly fool a few of your friends – because they are dull and dim-witted (only joking!). Get them together and dictate this multiplication:

1 times 2
    times 3
        times 4
           times 5
                times 6
                    times 7
                        times 8
                            times 9
                              times 0

The first of your friends to give you the correct answer is the winner. (Which is 0 of course, but you knew that anyway!)

Here at Brandreth Towers we love a
good party. And nothing makes a good party
go better than a great party game. Here are
some of the very greatest. From Blind Man's
Buff to Wink Murder, hosts and hostesses
will find games for all ages and occasions.
Browse through and choose the ones best
suited to the particular mood and maturity of
your guests.
For ease of reference, we have divided
the games in this chapter into two parts:
Children's Party Games and Dinner and
After-Dinner Games. But don't let that
restrict you: there is no good reason why the
adults shouldn't enjoy a round of Squeak
Piggy Squeak if they are so inclined.

CHILDREN'S PARTY GAMES

• • •

It was at the parties of our childhoods that many of us first encountered good old-fashioned organised fun. Of course, in days gone by, the music for Musical Bumps was provided by cousin Catherine bashing out Chopsticks on an out-of-tune upright rather than courtesy of the latest MP3 player plugged into the computer dock. But, rest assured, even if the technology of the support systems has changed over the years, the fun levels on offer remain the same.

Jelly, ice cream and hats on a piece of elastic at the ready . . . it's party time!

Rory says: I love *all* these games. Party on, dude . . .

Saethryd and Gyles say: Back in Pippa mode for a moment, we have found when organising children's parties that it is the responsibility of the adults involved to set the pace.

With very young children it is generally not wise to have more than two or three organised games; it is better to provide a selection of toys for the little ones to play with most of the time. With older children one must be careful not to let the fun get out of hand. Children usually love the more active and boisterous games, but it is best to intersperse them with some quieter ones. Otherwise, with too much hilarity and excitement, it *will* all end in tears.

Be on hand to make sure that nothing gets broken or damaged (including the children!), but try not to fence the kids in with too much caution: it is a party, after all. Try to achieve a happy balance and the children will enjoy themselves . . . and so will you.

All Change

All the players except one sit in a circle on the floor. Blindfold the remaining player and stand him in the middle of the circle. Then ask all the seated players to choose the names of well-known towns or cities for themselves. One will be London, another Cardiff, another Edinburgh, and so on. Each player must announce the town of their choice and no two players can be the same town.

To begin the game the conductor, who is standing outside the circle and can't take part, aka Mum or Dad, picks out two towns sitting on opposite sides of the circle and calls out 'The train is now going from London to Leeds' – or from Plymouth to Perth, or Brighton to Birmingham, as the case may be. The two towns must now get up and change places, while the blindfolded player standing in the middle of the circle tries to catch hold of one of them as they pass.

If he succeeds, the captured player has to put on the blindfold and the player who has been in the middle can sit down and choose the name of a town for himself.

If, after a few changeovers, no one has been caught, the leader calls 'All change!' and *everyone* has to cross to the other side of the circle – in which case the player in the middle is certain to catch someone!

Blind Postman

Here's a variation on All Change. One player is chosen to be the postman and is blindfolded. The other players sit in a circle with the postman standing in the middle. Each of the seated players is given the name of a town. The postman calls out the names of two towns and those two players have to exchange seats while the postman attempts to occupy one of the temporarily available seats. Whoever loses their seat becomes the postman.

Blind Man's Buff

T his is one of the oldest games in history and has been played all over the world for thousands of years.

One player is chosen to be the Blind Man and is blindfolded. The other players lead her to the middle of the room, turn her round three times in each direction, and then leave her on her own.

The Blind Man tries to catch one of the other players, while they move about the room, calling to her and taunting her, approaching as near as they dare and dodging away again.

A player who is touched by the Blind Man must immediately stand still. If, by touching and feeling, the Blind Man can say who it is she has caught, then the captured player becomes the Blind Man for the next round of the game. If the Blind Man guesses wrongly the name of the captured player, then she must let him go and carry on trying to catch another player.

Saethryd says: If you think Blind Man's Buff is a tricky game to play in Britain in the second decade of the twenty-first century, think yourself lucky that you didn't live in ancient Japan, where the girls played it wearing full kimonos and carrying a cup of tea from which they weren't allowed to spill a drop.

Cat and Mouse

One player is chosen to be the cat and is blindfolded. Another player is chosen to be the mouse. The remaining players form a circle, with the cat and the mouse standing in the middle.

The cat has to try to catch the mouse by following the sound of his voice. At any time the cat can stand still and call 'Miaow'. The mouse must then reply, 'Squeak, squeak', but can immediately run, creep or tiptoe to another part of the circle. When the mouse is caught he becomes the cat for the next round and another player is chosen to be the mouse.

Chinese Whispers

Chinese Whispers is known as Telephone in America and it was originally called Russian Scandal here in Great Britain.

Everyone sits in a circle and, when the game begins, one player (the birthday boy or girl, perhaps) is told to whisper a secret message to the person sitting on their right. The message can only be whispered once and should be short and, even, a bit silly. The second player has to pass on what he's heard – or what he *thinks* he's heard – to the third player, and so the whispering goes on until the message has been right round the group, when the last player announces the message he or she received and the first player reveals the message actually sent out. Very rarely do they turn out to be the same!

There is a fun pencil-and-paper version of this game that can be played by budding artists. It works best with the players sitting around a table. The first person whispers the name of an object, person or thing to the player sat on their right – a dog, a kettle, the Queen. The second player then has to *draw* said object on a piece of paper. When they have finished they fold the piece of paper and pass it to the person on their right, who opens it and, on a separate piece of paper, draws what they think they can see. It is very important that subsequent players don't see the artistic efforts of the players before them. You will be amazed how the object changes by the time it gets to the last player. And, unlike the spoken version, you will have a trail showing how the transformation has taken place.

The Chocolate Game

This game is always a big hit at parties. You will need a dice, a big bar of chocolate (or two or three, depending on how many children you have and how much they love chocolate, which in our experience tends to be a *lot*), a knife and fork, a hat, a scarf and a pair of gloves.

Get all the children to sit in a circle and put the chocolate and bits and bobs in the centre on a tray. The first player throws the dice and then passes it to the next player who throws it, then the next, and so on round in a circle until someone throws a six. When that happens, whoever is lucky enough to throw the six leaps up, races to the centre of circle, where they have to put on the hat, scarf and gloves. They can then start eating the chocolate – but they have to eat it using the knife and fork.

While all this is going on, the other players are still rolling the dice. When another six is rolled, the player in the centre must put down the knife and fork, take off the bits and bobs and pass them over the next eager child, who will have raced to the centre to have their turn at the delicious goodies.

Thirsty Cat

This amusing variation on the Chocolate Game involves none of the dressing up but lots of make-believe. All you need is a tray, a dice and a bowl of juice. Play the game as above, but when a player throws a six, instead of getting to feast on yummy chocolate they have to crawl to the middle of the circle on all fours and start lapping up the juice from the bowl like a thirsty cat. They have to keep going till another player throws a six.

Rory says: This game is hilarious!

Clothes Shop

This is a funny, silly game that children of all ages love playing as they get to dress up and act the fool. In order to play, first fill a cardboard box with old clothes: you will need quite a lot. It's best to include a variety of styles, shapes and sizes: hats, gloves, shoes, jumpers, dresses, Grandpa's pyjamas, socks – the more ridiculous the better.

At the start of the game take as many items out of the box as there are children, less one (if you have eight children, pull out seven items of clothing) and pop them in a pile at one end of the room and get all the children to line up at the other.

When you shout 'Opening Hours!' all the children have to race to the pile, grab an item of clothing, put it on and race back to the start. One child will be left with nothing to wear. They then go to the box and choose the next lot of items to place at the end of the room, again one less than the number of children still left in, and the next round commences.

The winner is the child left claiming the last piece of clothing by which time they will be piled up high in old clothes.

Dusty Miller

This is one of the messiest and most marvellous of all party games. In order to play you will need a bowl, some flour and six twopenny pieces.

To protect the furniture and the carpet, cover the floor with a large sheet. In the middle of the sheet place a large bowl half filled with flour. Mixed up with the flour will be six well-scrubbed twopenny pieces. The players have got to kneel by the bowl, their arms folded behind their backs, and fish out as many coins as they can using only their teeth. The silly players will bury their faces in flour. The bright ones will simply *blow* at the flour until a coin is unearthed, when they will pick it up between their teeth. Whichever method is used, a good time will be had by all.

Goodies and Baddies

To play this game you will need two balloons – something not normally in short supply at children's parties.

The players are divided into two teams. One team, the Goodies, attempts to keep a balloon up in the air while the other team, the Baddies, attempts to burst it using only their hands and feet – pins and other such-like weapons of destruction are outlawed.

When the balloon has eventually been burst, the teams swap roles and play with the second balloon.

Handshake

One of the players is 'it'. The others stand in a circle, facing inwards, with their hands behind their backs. The player who is 'it' runs around the outside of the circle, slaps the hands of one of the players, and carries on running. The player whose hands were slapped runs around the circle in the opposite direction. When they meet they shake hands and then race back to the vacant space in the circle. The one who gets there last is 'it' for the next round.

Happy Travellers

For this game all the children will need a newspaper. The players sit in two rows, facing one another with their knees touching, and squashed together like passengers on a very crowded commuter train. (Bowler hats and umbrellas are optional.) Each player has a folded newspaper which has been thoroughly muddled up, with pages in the wrong order, some being back to front and some upside down. On the word of command, each player tries to arrange the pages of his newspaper into the correct order as quickly as possible. The first to succeed is the winner.

Hunt the Slipper

The players sit in a circle on the floor with one player sitting in the middle with the slipper. The player in the middle hands the slipper to one of the players around the circle, then covers his eyes and recites this rhyme:

Cobbler, cobbler, mend my shoe,
Have it done by half past two.
Cobbler, cobbler, tell me true,
Which of you has got my shoe?

While the player in the middle is reciting, the players around the circle pass the slipper from one to another behind their backs. Whoever is holding the slipper when the last word of the rhyme is uttered holds on to it, being careful to keep it out of sight. The player in the middle has two tries to guess who is holding the slipper. If he guesses correctly, the player holding the slipper goes into the middle for the next round.

Lost Letters

All the children except for one sit down in a circle. Give one child, the 'letter writer', an envelope – preferably a large, brightly coloured one (because that's more fun) – that's been filled with paper (because that stops it floating about).

The children in the circle all shut their eyes, and as the child with the envelope walks around them, they begin to chant:

> I wrote a letter to my love
> And on the way I dropped it.
> One of you has picked it up
> And put it in your pocket.

The moment they finish saying 'pocket' the letter writer drops the 'love letter' and all the other children look behind them to see if it is they that have the envelope. If it is, they must leap up and try and run round the circle and get back safely into their place before the letter writer catches them. If they are caught they take the place of the letter writer, if they make it home safely the letter writer stays on for another round.

The Mummy Game

A ll kids love ancient Egypt and it is that kind of mummy – not the type that tucks you into bed and tells you to clean your face – that this game refers to.

Everyone splits into pairs and each pair is given a full roll of loo paper. Within the pair, they must decide who is to be the mummy and who the mummifier.

A whistle blows and the pairs have three minutes, within which time the mummifier has to use the toilet paper to swathe her partner from head to foot so that he resembles an Egyptian mummy. The couple who are judged to have made the best mummy are the winners.

Rory says: Did you know in ancient Egypt they used to pull people's brains out through their noses when they were mummifying them? Which is gross . . . but awesome . . .

Musical Bumps

This is similar to Musical Chairs, except that the chairs are not required. While the music is playing the children skip, dance and jump up and down. When the music stops the children drop down to sit cross-legged on the floor. The last one to do so is eliminated. This is repeated until only one player is left. They are the winner.

Musical Chairs

No children's party at Osborne House in Queen Victoria's day was complete without a game of Musical Chairs. To play it you need one fewer chairs than there are players. Place the chairs side by side in alternate directions.

As the music plays the players dance around the chairs and the moment the music stops everyone has to sit down; that is, all but one. Whoever fails to find a seat drops out of the game, taking one chair with them. The music keeps on starting and stopping until there are just two players left cavorting round a single chair, and when the music stops for the last time, the player who manages to get into the chair first is the winner.

Musical Hats

All the players but one are given paper hats and they sit in a circle with their legs crossed. As soon as the music starts the players pass the hats around the circle. When the music stops, all those with a hat put them on their heads and the player without a hat drops out.

As each player drops out, he should take a hat with him. The last one left is the winner. Hats off to them!

Musical Statues

While the music is playing the children must dance about the room, moving continually. Encourage the children to really go for it and throw some groovy shapes on the floor. As soon as the music stops they must freeze in whatever position they happen to be in at that moment and must remain as still as statues. Anyone who moves is out. The music is restarted and the children continue dancing. The game continues in this manner until only one player is left in, and that player is the winner.

Saethryd says: For more musical merry-making see Chapter 7 coming up next.

On and Off

An old blanket is spread out on the floor. When the leader calls 'Everybody off the blanket' the children stand on the blanket, and when the leader calls 'Everybody on the blanket' they all get off, always doing the opposite of what the leader tells them. Any player who makes a mistake is out, and the last player left in is the winner.

Pairs Treasure Hunt

This game works well when you have a bit of time to prepare and not *too* many guests. If you have older family members around, perhaps you can get them to help out with the prep. If your party is for very young children – under four – keep your treasure hunt to just one room. If the children are a bit older then you can be a little bit more adventurous and go further afield.

Before the party starts go round the house and collect pairs of a number of small things – buttons, pens, stamps, tea bags, packets of sugar, chess pieces – anything you can think of. Prepare a small bag for each child – a party bag works well – and put five or six halves of the pairs in each bag. Hide the matching pair somewhere round the room or house. When it's time to play, give each child a bag and send them off for the hunt.

The first child who finds the matching pair for each item and gets a complete set is the winner.

Pass the Orange

There were no oranges, only apples, in the Garden of Eden, so we can be sure that Adam and Eve never played this game, which is a shame because they missed out on a total classic. You can play this game in a circle but if, like us, you prefer your games with a competitive edge, you can divide into two teams and turn it into race.

Each team forms a line and is given an orange. (If you are playing with really small children, a tangerine sometimes does the trick.) The aim of the game is to pass the piece of fruit from one end of the team to the other without using your hands at all. In fact, the fruit must be passed from chin to chin! The leader can use her hands to put it under her chin to begin with, but from then on it can only be passed from chin to chin. If it falls to the ground then the person passing it must pick it up and tuck it under their chin again before attempting to pass it on.

Pass the Parcel

A stalwart of children's parties everywhere, Pass the Parcel remains a perennial favourite, and deservedly so.

In preparation for the game, a fun little gift is wrapped in layers and layers of tissue, wrapping or newspaper, each layer being fastened with either string or adhesive tape.

The players all sit in a circle, and while the music is playing they pass the parcel from hand to hand as quickly as possible. The music is stopped abruptly at frequent intervals, and when this happens the player holding the parcel at that moment unwraps one layer of paper. The player who is lucky enough to unwrap the final layer wins the present.

It is a nice idea to put small sweets in between the layers as an extra treat (tape these to the outside of the next layer). Sometimes we also put forfeits in some of the layers, which adds to the drama and excitement of the game but does hold up the proceedings.

Plate and Feather Race

Earnest, the Brandreth family budgie, is never to be found when a round of the Plate and Feather Race is in the offing. This is because, as well as being quick of wing, he is no bird-brain. Earnest has cottoned on to the fact that for this game each player needs a paper plate and a feather. So while he has managed to maintain his magnificent plumage over the years, the feather duster in the cupboard under the stairs is starting to look a bit ropey.

The competitors line up at one end of the room, and each is given a feather on a paper plate. Carrying their plates, they have to race to the other end of the room and back again. A competitor whose feather comes off their plate must stop to put it back again, but otherwise no competitor must touch the feather: anyone who does so is sent back to the start.

Simon Says

One of the players is chosen to be the leader. The other players space themselves out in front of him. The leader performs various actions (such as standing on one leg, patting his head, raising his left arm, bending down) and commands the other players to do the same. If he begins the command with the words 'Simon says' – for example, 'Simon says, touch your toes' – then the other players must obey the command. If the command does not begin with the words 'Simon says' – for example, 'Touch your toes' – then the other players must not perform that action. A player who makes a mistake or who hesitates for too long before doing what Simon says drops out of the game.

The last player left in is the winner, and he becomes the leader for the next round.

Sleeping Lions

This game, also known as Dead Lions, is ideal for calming down boisterous little ones. It really is perfect for when you need a bit of peace and quiet; or if you just fancy a bit of a lie-down.

The players lie face down on the floor and pretend to be dead lions. Any player who makes the slightest movement is eliminated, and the last player left in is the winner.

The players who have been eliminated may help spot movements made by the remaining dead lions, and they may 'encourage' the lions to move by taunting them or trying to make them laugh, but no touching is allowed.

Squeak Piggy Squeak

This game is suitable only for very young children or for very sophisticated adults.

One player is blindfolded, and is given a cushion to hold. She is turned round, three times in each direction. The other players sit around her in a circle.

The blindfold player makes her way to one of the players seated in the circle, places her cushion on that player's lap, and sits on it. She calls out 'Squeak, piggy, squeak', and the player being sat upon has to squeak like a pig. If the blindfold player can identify the person whose lap she is sitting on, then the two players change places and the sat-upon player is blindfolded for the next round. Otherwise the blindfold player goes off to seek another lap.

Three Blind Mice

One of the players is chosen to be the Farmer's Wife. The other players join hands to form a circle around the Farmer's Wife, and then dance around her, singing:

> Three blind mice. Three blind mice.
> See how they run. See how they run.
> They all run after the Farmer's Wife,
> Who cut off their tails with a carving knife,
> Did you ever see such a thing in your life
> As three blind mice?

As the last word is sung, the players scatter and run to the walls of the room, while the Farmer's Wife tries to catch one of them. A player is 'safe' once he touches a wall. The first player to be caught becomes the Farmer's Wife for the next round of the game.

DINNER AND AFTER-DINNER GAMES

• • •

From grown-up word games ideal
for livening up the cheese course to seriously
silly after-dinner entertainments, the
following selection of games is guaranteed
to make any evening go with a swing.

Ad Infinitum

This game is the answer to your problem when the dinner party conversation starts to flag.

The host or hostess acts as umpire and needs to have their watch and their wits at the ready. Each guest must talk for thirty seconds, without hesitation or repetition, and at the end of allotted period their neighbour must immediately pick up the story and continue it, without ever bringing it to a conclusion. Anyone who pauses, repeats himself or apparently ends the story is out. The last person talking is the winner and, as their reward, can end the story in exactly the way they want.

The umpire decides when a pause is not a pause, a repetition is not a repetition, and an ending is not an ending. And the umpire's decision is final!

The umpire can also choose the title for the story and pick the player who must begin it. He must keep an eye on his watch and tell each player when his or her half-minute is up.

All Lies

Mark Twain once said: 'If you tell the truth, you don't have to remember anything.'

Surprising as it may sound, attempting to tell the truth is actually easier than trying to tell lies, and this game requires the players *never* to speak the truth. For the length of the starter, pudding or main, the truth is impermissible. In the course of conversation, if any guest suspects another guest of having told the truth, he should report the truthful guest to the host, who will oblige the guilty guest to undertake a forfeit – most probably an impersonation of Pinocchio.

Breath Test

O ne London host is known to ask his guests to walk down a straight white line before they drive off home at the end of the evening. If they seem unsteady, the host sends them home by taxi and gets his chauffeur to drive their cars after them. If you don't happen to have a white line painted on your drawing-room floor or a chauffeur who lives in, this game is a good substitute. In a jolly sort of way, it has a sobering effect on those who play it and is a good, quick game with which to wind up a party.

The players stand in a circle, each armed with a mug of black coffee, a hunk of cheddar cheese and an unblown balloon. On the word 'Go!' players must gulp down the coffee, consume the cheese and blow up the balloon till it bursts. The first person to do this is the most sober and has won. Apart from its anti-alcoholic effects, established by experience, if not yet by scientific experiment, the game is guaranteed to make the party end with a bang.

Busy Birds

This game will go down well at your dinner party if your guests are big kids. It is an adaptation of a classic children's party game and is designed to be played at the table. It is best played after dinner (and a few drinks) by people who don't take themselves too seriously.

Each player must place their right hand on their left arm. When everyone is in position, you will tell them a story. It will be a story about all sorts of birds and beasts. Whenever you mention the name of a bird – a sparrow or a parrot, for example – the players should all raise their right hands and flutter them in the air. Whenever you mention birds in general, all the players must flutter both hands in the air. But whenever you mention the name of an animal that cannot fly, the players right hands must remain firmly on their left arm. When a player makes a mistake, he or she has to drop out of the game. Of course, the more complicated the story you tell, the more confused the players will get and the more fun will be had by all.

Here's an example of the kind of story you could tell.

I woke up very early this morning. Outside my window, the birds were singing (all hands up) and so, after I had fed my pet budgie Earnest (right hands up) and given the cat (nobody moves) some milk, I went out into the garden. The birds (all hands up) were making a wonderful noise and on the lawn a starling (right hands up) and a sparrow (right hands still up) were fighting over a worm (nobody moves) . . .

Carry on with the story, mentioning as many birds and animals as you can think of, until there is only one player left. That player is the winner, and gets out of helping with the washing-up.

Candles

This is a fun game to play at the end of dinner. Move the chairs aside and make sure you have a lit candle on the table. Guests take it in turns. Blindfold the first player, revolve them twice, tell them to take three steps back and three steps forward and get them to blow out the candle with their arms folded behind their back. The players who succeed get prizes. (Don't worry, you won't run short of prizes: the challenge is far trickier than it sounds.)

The Cereal Box Game

After dinner isn't traditionally the time for cereal. It is, however, the *ideal* time to play the Cereal Box Game. All you need are a bunch of flexible friends, an empty cereal box and a pair of scissors.

The cereal box is placed on the floor in the middle of the room. The aim of the game is to pick up the cereal box using only your mouth and with only your feet touching the ground – so no kneeling, lying on the floor or using your hands for balance. Players take it in turn. If a player fails to pick up the box, they are eliminated.

Once everyone has had a turn, an inch is cut off the top of the box and another round is played. Everyone has another attempt – some will fail, some will succeed. Then another inch is cut off and another round played. The game goes on in this fashion until either one player is left victorious or the cereal box is a mere millimetre high.

Saethryd says: Popular techniques in the Cereal Box Game include the classic hands clasped behind the back and bend from the waist manoeuvre and the more experimental one-legged lunge. Those with exceptionally good balance might try the Cossack dancer's squat or even the wide-kneed frog position.

Doasyouwouldbedoneby

The Victorian writer Charles Kingsley described his creation, Mrs Doasyouwouldbedoneby, the water babies' friend, as 'the loveliest fairy in the world'. The host and hostess who regularly play this game on their guests deserve no such accolade. It is a mean game, not enjoyed by many, yet it is still quite popular in certain parts of north London.

Before the guests arrive the host must prepare name cards for everyone who is expected. The cards are separated according to gender and those bearing the names of the male guests are placed in one box while those carrying the women's names are placed in another.

When it is time to play the game, have each woman draw a man's card and each man draw a woman's card. Now instruct everyone to write on the card some action, stunt, exhibition or form of indoor entertainment he or she would like to see performed.

Naturally everybody will assume that the person named on the card will be expected to do the dirty work, although nothing to that effect has been said. But – Ho! Ho! Surprise! Surprise! – instead of collecting the cards and passing them to the persons named thereon, the host will ask each player in turn to read out what he or she has written on the card and will then say, 'If that's what you want, let's see *you* do it.' So the hapless Judy who wanted Richard to rub noses with the hostess now has to do it herself. And the luckless David who visualised Victoria performing

Gangnam Style must undertake the desperately embarrassing deed himself.

This means the nice guests who really do do as they would be done by, come off quite lightly. It is only to the horrid ones that the whirligig of time brings in his revenges.

Guess the Guests

This is a delicious psychological game that involves a little pre-party homework.

Before everyone arrives for dinner the host must prepare a written outline of the personality traits of each guest. The guests aren't named but *numbered* in this psychological portrait gallery, and when they arrive for the festivities they are each given a copy of all the personality portraits.

At the end of the evening everyone is invited to produce the list, and, having studied the descriptions and met their fellow guests, fit the actual names to the numbers. The game will only work if the host in writing these psychological biographies has been honest with himself and his friends.

The Judge

This is a good game to play when you've got a few close friends, preferably couples, over for dinner. It is only too easy to imagine the Camerons, the Wade-Brookses and the rest of the Chipping Norton set playing a happy round or two over a cosy kitchen supper.

One player, usually the host, is chosen to act as the judge, while all the other players divide into pairs. The game works best when the pairs are people who know each other well. The judge turns to a couple and asks one of them a question. Whoever the Judge questions, it is that person's *partner* who must reply. So for example, if David were asked 'What is your favourite pastime?', Samantha would, no doubt, reply 'Chillaxing'. Anyone who speaks when he is spoken to or doesn't answer when his partner is questioned has to drop out and so does the player he is paired with.

A lot of fun can be had with this game if the judge is a clever one, because they can ask the sort of questions they know the players are longing to answer for themselves but mustn't.

Limbo

The limbo originated on the island of Trinidad. It is a form of dance, in which the dancer dances their way under a limbo pole that gets progressively closer to the ground. It is the most fun when played to music, with the other players chanting the classic 'How low can you go? How low can you go?' refrain at the hapless contestant trying to bend as far backwards as possible without falling over.

It's best to move to the living room before embarking on a round of limbo. This is an energetic, loud and raucous game (if played properly) and has prompted a few complaints from the neighbours here at Brandreth Towers in its time. The variant we play is called Broom Limbo. This is because we do not have a dedicated limbo pole and so a broom does the job nicely instead.

Two players hold the broom horizontally at chest height so that it acts as a bar. The other players line up and take it in turns to 'limbo' under it. To limbo correctly, you must bend backwards to get under the bar. You may not touch the bar or the ground, nor may you bend forward. If a player does any of these things they are disqualified.

Once all the players are through to the other side, the broom is lowered and the remaining players limbo through again. This process is repeated, with the broom being lowered each time, till one player is left victorious.

In Trinidad, the limbo started out as a dance performed at funeral wakes. Occasionally, when played in Britain by those of riper years with weak backs, it does end it tears.

Match Tower

This matchstick game makes for a fun after-dinner pastime, requiring as it does an empty bottle with a narrow neck, such as a wine bottle. If the only available wine bottle is full, it is not a good idea to drink the contents in order to play: this game calls for a steady hand.

The number of matches required for the game depends on the dexterity of the players. For clumsy players, only a few dozen matches will be needed, while expert players may need several hundred. The aim is to build up layer after layer of matches over the mouth of the bottle, each player in turn adding one match. The first four matches are laid across the mouth of the bottle, the next four are laid across the previous four, and so on.

There are no winners, but the loser is the player who first dislodges the structure and sends it tumbling down. He must pay whatever penalty is decided by the other players.

Never Say It

This is the dinner-party version of Taboo (page 234).

You announce to all the players that, for the length of the cheese course, certain common words must not be spoken. Good words to choose are 'I', 'Yes' and 'No'. Anyone caught uttering the forbidden words must immediately get up from the table and start on the washing-up.

Over the Sticks

This is a fun one when you have a large group round for dinner. It's less of a game and more of a jape, and half of your guests will be in on the trick with you . . .

While everyone is finishing up in the kitchen or dining room, you will need to pop into the living room to prepare. Arrange as many upright chairs as appropriate in two facing rows down the centre of the room with a little passageway down the middle.

Half the party are now brought in to sit on the chairs facing each other so that their feet are just touching. Two more guests are now brought in and are made to stand at the start of the line of chairs. They are allowed to look at the positions of the feet of the people who are sitting down. They are then blindfolded and instructed to walk down the line, taking care to step over the feet of the others.

Just as they are setting off on their journey, the seated players silently draw in their feet, so that as the couple walks down the line they are trying to avoid something that isn't there. When the couple have got to the end of the line and are congratulating themselves on their skillful navigation, they are unmasked and told what has happened. Two more players are brought in and (we hope) fooled the same way.

The advent of camera phones has made this game even more entertaining. Be sure to record the hapless duo as they tentatively make their way between the chairs. Then they can look back and laugh along with the other guests who have been stifling their titters so as not to give the game away.

The Pen in the Bottle Game

This is a ridiculous after-dinner game much loved by the Sloane Rangers in their day (the 1980s). You can just imagine the horsey girls in pearls guffawing away as Hugo, Tarquin and old-what's-his-chops gyrated hopelessly next to the dinner table. No doubt its legacy lives on at the dinner parties of Fulham and Chelsea in the teens of the twenty-first century.

The game is very simple. Tie a piece of string round a pen or pencil; then tie that piece of string round the waist of your competitor so that it is dangling down a few inches/cm or so. The game is usually played one by one, as this gives the assembled guests more a chance to chuckle at the player's antics. A bottle, usually a wine bottle, is placed beneath the player and the aim of the game is to try and get the pencil into the bottle. It is not the most sophisticated of games but, truth be told, it does always raise a giggle or seven.

Personality Swap

This game is not without risks (of all kinds) and is only to be played with the right people. If played with any honesty, it can be grimly revealing.

For the length, say, of the soup course, guests must swap personalities with the person sitting opposite and behave in exactly the way they believe the person facing them would behave. Naturally the better the guests know each other the more devastating the results. And when played by a couple having dinner *à deux*, the effect can be shattering.

The Picture Frame Game

This is a simple, silly game which, nevertheless, calls for great self-control. It's an excellent game to play while guests are waiting for their taxis, because you can get up and go in the middle and spoil nobody's fun.

The assembled company forms a circle and individuals are required to hold a huge and empty picture frame in front of their faces for two minutes without moving a muscle, while the other players cavort and caper and grimace and call out ribald remarks. If the framed player's face so much as flickers, he gives up the frame, loses a point and/or has to undertake a forfeit.

Poor Pussy

This is a ridiculous game that isn't nearly as easy as it sounds. It was originally a children's game, but we find it works a treat as a somewhat surreal after-dinner jape. (Just make sure George Galloway isn't on the guest list.)

All the players sit or stand in a circle. One player draws the short straw and is chosen to go into the middle to be the pussy cat. The pussy cat, on hands and knees, goes to each player in turn, purring and miaowing. When the frisky feline approaches a player and miaows, that player has to stroke or pat the cat who is kneeling at his feet and say 'Poor Pussy!' three times while keeping a straight face. No smiling, smirking, giggling and definitely no laughing are allowed. If the approached player stays stony-faced, the pussy moves on to his or her next victim. If a whisper of amusement appears on the player's face, it's their turn to play at being Oscar, Felix, Squash or Mr Tiddles.

What Nonsense!

This game requires each player to talk a lot of nonsense about a particular topic for two minutes.

A list of topics is devised – as many topics as there are players – and each topic is written on a slip of paper, which is then folded. The topics can be fairly straightforward, for example:

1. New uses for old chocolate
2. Teaching goldfish to talk
3. Did aliens build the Great Wall of China?
4. Why is a raven like a writing-desk?

Or they may be just a little more rarefied, like these:

5. Is it Wednesday in Bolivia?
6. The answer that cannot be questioned
7. If not, why not?
8. The functionalism of inverse dichotomy

Each player in turn chooses a slip at random and then has to speak for two minutes on the topic chosen. The person who attains the highest peaks of lunacy is the winner.

Wink Murder

On sitting down for dinner, all the guests take a card from a bowl in the middle of the table. All but one of the cards will be blank. One will have a cross on it. The guest who draws that card is the murderer.

The aim of the game is for the murderer to kill as many of his fellow guests as possible before he or she is outed as the homicidal lunatic at the table. The murderer kills off his fellow guests by surreptitiously winking at them. The murder victim must then count to five before screaming and announcing their untimely death.

In the classic version of the game, all the other players are trying to catch the murderer. If a fellow guest thinks they know who it is, they point at their suspect and say 'I accuse you of murder'. If they have correctly guessed the guilty party, they have won the game. If they have guessed incorrectly, they are out. If no one guesses the identity of the murderer before the end of dinner, the murderer wins.

An alternative version of this game involves having one murderer and one detective. Two marked cards will be placed in the bowl: one with a cross and one with a circle. The player who draws the circle card publicly declares it. They will be the detective. The game continues as above, except that the only player trying to guess the murderer's identity is the detective, which means our dining-table dealer of death can be less discreet as he winks at the other players.

Saethryd says: On Hallowe'en we like to play a fun variation of this game called Vampire Murder. The rules are exactly the same as Wink Murder, the difference being that the murderer tops his victims by baring his teeth at them!

Music & DRAMA

The games presented in this chapter are a pick and mix of musical and dramatic delights, suitable for drama queens (kings and princes) of all ages, tastes and talents. Try a round of Corpse Tango after a raucous dinner at home, or the Conductor on a Saturday afternoon with friends, family and Great-Aunt Beryl. Fairy Tales is for the more sophisticated thespians among you, Musical Islands is for the kids and Balloon Dance . . .? Well, Balloon Dance is for everybody.

Adverbs

This is a fun game that can be played with any number of players.

One person is chosen to leave the room. While that person is outside the rest of the players decide on a descriptive adverb – whatever they like, from the everyday ('happily') to the unusual ('ostentatiously'). Once the adverb has been chosen, the outsider returns. He then asks each of the other players, in turn, to perform an action. It could be reading the paper, say, or singing, taking a shower, playing tennis or hailing a cab. The challenge is that each player must perform their given action in the style of the adverb the group has chosen. When each player has done their bit, it is time for the outsider to guess what the adverb is.

You can play the game two ways. If you would like to keep score, you get 3 points if you guess the adverb correctly first time, 2 points if you guess on your second attempt and 1 point if you guess on your third. The player with the most points at the end of however many rounds you chose to play is the winner. Alternatively, you can simply play so that if the outsider fails to uncover the adverb, then he must perform a forfeit. It's up to you.

Gyles says: The less obvious the adverb the more entertaining the game tends to be. For example, if one of the players were tasked with leaving the room 'clumsily' or 'quickly', it wouldn't take much for the outsider to guess what they were doing. If it is something more ingenious – say 'rumbunctiously', 'inquisitively' or 'Germanically' – the challenge to the outsider (and the amusement of the rest) is that much greater.

Here are some adverbs to get you in the mood . . . Mmm . . . 'moodily' is a good one.

AMIABLY	GRIMLY	PIOUSLY
BASHFULLY	HAPPILY	PLAINTIVELY
BEAUTIFULLY	HARSHLY	POLITELY
BRUTALLY	HOPEFULLY	POMPOUSLY
CHARMINGLY	HORRIBLY	ROMANTICALLY
CHEEKILY	HURRIEDLY	RUDELY
CRISPLY	HYSTERICALLY	SADLY
CURTLY	JEALOUSLY	SARCASTICALLY
DELIBERATELY	KINDLY	SLOWLY
DEMONIACALLY	LAUGHINGLY	SOFTLY
DEVOTEDLY	LUSTFULLY	SPONTANEOUSLY
EMOTIONALLY	MAGNIFICENTLY	SURELY
EVENLY	MANFULLY	SWEETLY
FANATICALLY	METICULOUSLY	TRAGICALLY
FEEBLY	MOURNFULLY	TRUTHFULLY
FURIOUSLY	NICELY	VICIOUSLY
GLARINGLY	NOBLY	VIRTUOUSLY
GREGARIOUSLY	OFFICIOUSLY	WEAKLY

Avoid the Hassock

Did we hear you murmur 'What on earth is a hassock?' Although many people associate hassocks primarily with keeping their knees off the cold stone floor at church, technically a hassock is any firm cushion used for sitting or kneeling on, or as a foot-rest. For the purposes of this game, you do not have to have an actual hassock to hand; anything that you think would work – a firm pillow, sofa cushions, even a big stuffed toy – will do, just as long as it is not going to hurt you if you accidentally fall on it.

Here is how to play the game. Place a hassock on its end in the middle of the room and get the players to form small circle round it. When the music starts, they must link arms and dance around the hassock. The aim of the game is that every player should try to pull every other player over the hassock. As the players are pulled to and fro they will leap up and down and go back and forth in their attempt to avoid the hassock. Anyone who knocks over the hassock leaves the game. The last player left dancing round the standing hassock is the winner.

Balloon Dance

According to the *Oxford English Dictionary* a 'Paul Jones', a dance in which men and women swap partners after dancing in concentric circles, is named after a certain John Paul Jones, an eighteenth-century Scottish-born admiral. Unfortunately, the dictionary does not tell us *why*. One can only speculate as to whether John Paul was a whiz on the dance floor or whether his battle tactic was to circle his ships round the enemy's before launching an attack.

What we do know is that the Balloon Dance is the most entertaining version of a 'Paul Jones' you can imagine. Why? Because you do it with a balloon between your knees, of course.

It's a great game for a large crowd and it helps to have an even, or relatively even, ratio of men to women or boys to girls to start with. To save time, and your lungs, get everyone to blow up their own balloon, then have the women form a circle in the middle facing outwards and the men form a circle around them facing inwards. Balloons between the knees, please, and we are ready to start.

When the music plays, the circles perambulate in reverse directions and, when it stops, each man must approach the lady he happens to be facing and partner her for a brief dance.

The dance over, the circles reform and perambulate to the music once again. All this must be performed with balloons firmly between the knees. Anyone bursting or dropping their balloon is eliminated. Anyone stranded without a partner when the circulating music stops also drops out.

The last pair left dancing are the winners.

Rory says: I think I'd like this game because I like balloons and I *love* things that are hilarious. And this sounds like it would be hilarious. If only I knew what 'perambulate' meant . . . What? Oh, it's a fancy word for walk. Oh, okay, that would definitely be hilarious (especially if Grandpa B was playing).

Charades

'I think the worst time to have a heart attack is during a game of Charades'. So said US comedian Demetri Martin.

There is no finer party game, none more entertaining, none more popular than Charades. The word 'charade' is derived from the Spanish *charrada*, meaning the chatter of clowns, but it came to England and was transformed into a post-prandial indoor entertainment in 1776. Since then it has been one of our treasured national pastimes and no proper party is complete without it.

The first version of Charades described here is the traditional one, though it is the second version that has gained popularity in recent years, and this is what you are more likely to find being played in the living rooms of Loughborough, Loch Fyne and Llandaff.

Variation 1

Players are divided into teams, the first team retiring to another room, choosing a word which they are to dramatise and planning the performance they are to give. The chosen word must contain several syllables, each of which may be presented in the form of a dramatic sketch, as must the word as a whole. For example, the word 'trampoline' could be chosen and split into 'tramp' 'pole' and 'lean'. Or the chosen word might be illuminate, split up as 'ill', 'human' and 'ate'.

The captain then returns to the room and announces how many syllables there are in the word his team has chosen to dramatise and in what order the syllables are to be dramatised. The players return to the room and perform their sketches for the edification of the opposing team, acting out first the syllables and then the whole word. If they want, they may use speech in their sketches, but some people think it's more fun to have the sketches presented entirely in mime.

Variation 2

A popular variation of traditional Charades involves acting out the titles of books, films, TV programmes and songs.

In this form the titles are usually broken down into individual words and then into syllables if need be. This version is often played as a solo game with one player choosing and then acting out their chosen title for the assembled crowd to guess. Once the player who is acting out their chosen title has made a decision, the first thing they do is let the assembled gathering know whether it is a book, film, song or TV programme. Here's how this is done.

For Book, put your palms together and then open them as if they are the pages of a book.

For Film, curl your hands and hold one up to your eye as if it is a lens and with the other mark out an imaginary wheel near your ear, like you are using an old-fashioned cine camera.

For Song, mime your best opera moment.

For TV Programme, draw the shape of a TV screen with your forefingers.

Once that is established (there is normally much excited shouting and off-the-sofa leaping as players race to catch on to what is being described), you can start your mime.

For those of you who are completely new to the marvellous game that is Charades, here are a few more handy (pun-intended) gestures to get you on your way.

How many words? — Hold up as many fingers in the air as there are words in the title.

Which word are you miming? — Hold up first finger, second finger, and so on.

How many syllables? — Tap the amount of fingers as there are syllables against the inside of your elbow.

Which syllable are you miming? — Tap the first finger, second finger, and so on against the inside of your elbow.

Sounds like — Hold a hand cupped to the ear.

Small word — Make a mini-pincer gesture with your thumb and forefinger.

The word 'the' — Hold up forefingers at right angles to make a letter T.

The word 'and' — Hold up crossed forefingers to make the + symbol.

Saethryd says: These are just a few of the tips and tricks we use in our family. It may be that your family already has a complete repertoire of gestures and symbols handed down through the generations. If so, we'd LOVE to see them. Get in touch on Twitter or upload on the Facebook page #LOSTARTOFHAVINGFUN.

The Conductor

If your ambition is one day to be a great conductor – or a famous band leader, or if you just like to have a good time – this is the game for you. It's guaranteed to bring harmony to even the most discordant of gatherings.

Gather all the players together and get them to stand facing you. Then give to each of them an imaginary instrument: Aunty Beryl on the tuba, Cousin Johnny gets the double bass, the Gosling triplets from next door on the piccolos and your best mate Bob on the drums. (*Gyles says*: I like being the triangle, bing!) Now, let a dignified hush of anticipation fall over the auditorium, raise your (imaginary) baton and let the concert begin . . .

Here's how it works. As the conductor, you don't actually conduct; you clap your hands. The concert starts when you start clapping and, as you clap, the gathered ensemble must all begin to play their instruments, making the noise required to match their instrument. When you as the conductor stop clapping and begin to copy the movements of one of the players – drawing the bow across a violin, beating a drum, blowing a big trombone – all the other players, except the violinist or the drummer or the trombonist, must stop playing, so that you and one other player are left performing a duet.

As conductor, you can change instruments as often as you like and any player who carries on playing their instrument after you have changed to another one, or any player who fails to notice that you have swapped to their particular instrument, drops out.

To get the maximum fun out of the game, the conductor should change instruments as often as possible and bring his whole orchestra back in frequently by clapping his hands.

Corpse Tango

Corpse Tango is a slightly more grown-up version of Musical Statues (page 275). It can be played by adults and children alike and is particularly fun after a jolly dinner when everyone feels like letting loose and having a bit of a giggle.

The players dance the tango (or their best approximation of it) until the music stops, when they freeze completely in whatever position they happen to find themselves. The host and hostess then wander about doing their utmost – by means of funny faces and funnier remarks – to make the frozen figures twitch and snigger. The host and hostess may not touch the players and have only fifteen seconds or so in which to do their dirty work. Any player caught moving once the music has stopped joins the host and hostess in their attempt to get the corpses to betray signs of life. The music continues to stop and start until one victorious couple or player remains.

Saethryd says: Corpsing is a theatrical term which refers to the moment when an actor breaks character and starts laughing, sometimes uncontrollably. The term is said to have originated when japesters in an ensemble cast would endeavour to get the poor actors who were playing dead on stage to get the giggles, so ruining the most sombre and dramatic moments of the play.

Drama School

This is a fun game made all the more entertaining by its simplicity.
It can be played by budding Brad Pitts and Judi Denches anywhere and everywhere, whether waiting at the bus stop, on a family lunch out, frittering away a couple of hours in the park on a sunny afternoon or huddled at home hiding from the rain.

One player is chosen (or elects herself) to be the judge, and the other players sit or stand in a row facing her. The judge commands the players to express various moods or emotions – anger, despair, panic, delight, boredom, pride, fear, enthusiasm, benevolence, lust, incomprehension, smugness, guilt, and so on – and awards a point to the best actor of each mood or emotion. The winner is the player who amasses the most points.

The players may be allowed full scope to use speech, gesture and facial expression, or, to make it more difficult, they may be restricted to using facial expression only.

If you want to bump up the competitive edge, fashion yourself a fake Oscar to hand to the winner. But just be prepared for the speeches: 'I'd like to thank my mum and dad for making me, my agent and God – in that order. This one's for you, Grandma,' as the statue is held aloft and the tears start to fall.

Dumb Crambo

O ver three hundred years ago Samuel Pepys noted in his diary: 'From thence to The Hague, again playing at Crambo in the waggon.'

Anything Pepys could do, you should be able to do better. And Dumb Crambo is undoubtedly a better game than Crambo. (See page 213 for how to play Crambo and judge for yourself.) Here's how Dumb Crambo is played.

The players divide into two teams. Team A goes out of the room while the members of team B confer among themselves to choose a word. When team A returns, team B announce a word that *rhymes* with the word they have chosen. Team A is then allowed three guesses in which to discover the word of team B. The only restriction is that they are not allowed to speak: team A must present their guesses in mime.

Any player who speaks loses the game for their team; incorrect guesses are greeted with boos and hisses; and a correct guess is rewarded with applause and a point for the successful team. The teams alternate roles, and the team with the most points when no one wants to play any longer is the winner.

As mentioned above, Crambo can be played without the dumb-show, as it was until the eighteenth century, with team A simply guessing at the chosen word having heard another word that rhymes with it, but, here at Brandreth Towers, we are firmly of the belief that it is the mime which gives the game its bite.

Fairy Tales

This is a marvellous game to play with a largish group and can take up a whole afternoon if you really throw yourself into it: costumes, scripts, intervals, the whole shebang. Equally, it can be just as much fun dashed off in five fabulous minutes of glorious improvisation.

Players divide into two teams and each team is given a famous fairy tale to re-enact. *But* they must assume their dramatic roles, not as themselves, but as well-known personalities of the day. So were *Little Red Riding Hood* the tale of one team's choice, the part of Red Riding Hood might be played by Beyoncé, the Wolf by David Cameron and the Woodcutter by Eddie Izzard. Once the first team has performed its tale, the opponents must guess which fairy story it was and the double identity of all the players.

The game can be given an added twist by requiring the players to act their story in the manner of a particular film director. *Cinderella* à la Tarantino or *Chicken Little* through the eyes of Woody Allen both offer intriguing dramatic possibilities. Although it will take quite a performance to top Gyles' tour de force as Puss in Boots à la Silvio Berlusconi, which received rave reviews last Christmas.

Fancy Undress

A Fancy Undress Party is a Fancy Dress Party with a subtle difference. The guests are invited to come sporting not the clothes but the *personality* of a famous figure of fact or fiction. Adam comes dressed as he is but behaves like Robin Hood; Eve comes in a regular outfit but acts like she is Lady Gaga. At the end of the party (or after an hour or so, if guests are wearying of the game – an evening as George W. Bush or Madonna would tax anyone's inner resources) everyone must guess who everyone else was pretending to be.

The Common Man Game

Role-playing is said to be remarkably liberating and this variation is a simple role-playing game with a difference.

The guests are invited to the party, not as themselves but not as Napoleon or Brad Pitt or the Queen either. The game's only rule is that the players may not be themselves or anyone they know. They must be characters of their own creating – ordinary individuals – and they must act like their chosen characters to the life, supplying a name, family, career and complete historical and psychological background for themselves. If you had childhood fantasies of espionage and long to lose yourself in someone else's identity, this is the game for you.

Gyles says: Whenever I play this game, for reasons best known to my analyst, I choose to be a dentist from Ongar called Eric.

Grab

This is an eighteenth-century game unjustly neglected in recent years, perhaps because, in order to play it, you need to know a song that is nearly three hundred years old. To help the players learn the song, write up the words on a large sheet of paper and put it where everyone can see it.

Preparations done, it's on with the game . . .

All the players except one, who becomes the solitary leader, choose partners and, in pairs, they march nimbly round the room singing this traditional verse:

There was a jolly miller who lived by himself,
As the wheel went round he made his wealth.
One hand in the hopper, the other in the bag,
As the wheel went round he made a grab.

On the word 'grab', everyone must change partners and the leader attempts to grab a partner for himself. After the skirmish, whoever is left without a partner becomes the lonely miller for the next round.

You can make up a tune as you go along or, alternatively, the tune of the folk-song 'Villikens and his Dinah' will fit the words exactly. (You know the tune of 'Villikens and his Dinah', surely?)

Grand Chain

This is a good getting-to-know-you game, which involves every guest being given a balloon as they arrive. The balloons can be of various colours, provided there is at least a pair of balloons of each colour. The balloons are distributed at random, alternately to the men and the women.

When everyone has arrived, the guests then search out another guest with the same coloured balloon, who they will partner for Grand Chain.

Once all the guests have found a partner, they form a chain of pairs around the room – imagine ladies and gentleman dancing in formation in Tudor times or in a Jane Austen novel – holding hands and holding their balloons *between their knees*.

When the music starts, the whole company troops around the room, moving in time with the music, which varies from a slow waltz to Justin Timberlake to AC/DC. If anyone drops or bursts their balloon, the pair is eliminated.

The game continues till all but the winning pair have left the chain.

Group Limericks

A s we all know,

The limerick is furtive and mean,
You must keep her in close quarantine,
Or she sinks to the slums
And quickly becomes
Disgusting, revolting, obscene!

With this game, the responsibility for creating the limerick is shared. The
first player makes up the opening line of a limerick; the second player has
thirty seconds to come up with the next line; the third player another thirty
seconds for the third, and so on until the limerick is complete. The verse
does not need to make much sense, but it must rhyme and it should scan.

Here's an example of a group limerick created by five passengers flying
from Gatwick to Madrid shortly after they had been told the flight was being
diverted to Paris. It took them just thirty-five seconds to come up with this:

There was a young man on a plane
Who wanted to travel to Spain
But they led him a dance
And took him to France –
Next time he'll travel by train!

Group Poetry

If you feel the limerick as a form is beneath you – or too risky – you might like to try this game.

Each player writes down the first line of a verse (either somebody else's or an original composition), folds the paper over so that what he's written can't be seen, copies the last word below the fold and passes the paper to the player on his right, who now writes a second line to rhyme with the first. He too folds the paper, copies the last word and passes it to his right, when the whole process is repeated.

The end-product is a unique poem, which must be recited by each player with the requisite gravitas. It is not how Milton did it, nor indeed how Carol Ann Duffy does it, but it can be great fun all the same. And if you want to write modern poetry, don't bother with the rhyming. Just let the last word of each line 'inspire' the next line . . . and take the consequences.

Mimic

This is one of those games that is played more for laughs than for points. It's lots of fun to play round the dinner table or after a slap-up Sunday roast.

Before your guests arrive, prepare as many cards as you expect players. On each card write a brief description of a character, or the name of a well-known public figure.

If you suspect that your guests will not make marvellous mimics, you're best advised to put down simple descriptions such as 'News Reader', 'Village Busybody', 'Pompous Politician'. If you feel you've invited along a talented crowd, you can be more specific, listing the Queen and Mick Jagger, Michael Caine, Barbara Windsor, Michael McIntyre, Kermit the Frog and the like. (Don't put David Cameron on the list. Even a professional impressionist like Alistair McGowan says Cameron is impossible to mimic.)

When the time comes to play the game, each guest is given a nursery rhyme to recite – 'Humpty Dumpty' or 'Little Jack Horner' work well – and told to pick one of the specially prepared cards. (The traditional method, which ensures that players can't see what they are choosing, is to put all the cards in a hat and let players have a good rummage around before choosing. We have an old top hat at Brandreth Towers specifically for this purpose but a beanie hat, shoebox, pillowcase, or even a plastic bag from the supermarket, will work just as well.) The player then has to read the verse in the manner of the character named on the card, and the audience must guess who it is the player is mimicking.

Nobody wins, but a good time is had by all.

'WHEN THE MUSIC STOPS . . .'

• • •

The following six games are
all variations on a theme which will be
familiar to anyone who has ever attended,
or organised, a children's party. In fact,
in the children's party section in Chapter
6 above you will find a few more.

Musical Arches

Two pairs of players, one at each end of the room, stand with their hands joined above their heads to form an arch. All the other players line up in pairs and, as the music plays, dance through the two arches. When the music stops, the 'arches' drop their arms. If a pair is caught under an arch, that pair forms an arch itself. The game continues until all the pairs but one have been caught. The remaining pair are the winners.

Musical Arms

This is a jolly game for a large gathering who are blessed with buckets of energy and a generous dollop of co-ordination. You will need plenty of participants and plenty of space – room to swing about ten large ginger toms, by our reckoning.

The men stand in line, one behind another, in the centre of the room. The front player stands with his right hand on his hip, the other hand by his side; the second player has his left hand on his hip; the third player his right hand on his hip, and so on down the line.

The women, who should number one more than the men, dance around the line as the music plays and, as soon as it stops, they grab the arm of the nearest man. The one who fails to get an arm drops out, as does the first man in the queue. The game continues until there are just two vulture-like women left circling the last man. The winner is the one who successfully grabs the final arm.

Then it's the turn of the men to circle round the girls who stand in line.

Musical Islands

Prepare a number of large kidney- and liver-shaped islands from sheets of newspaper (or, if you are feeling a bit on the lazy side, just use the newspaper sheets as they are). Scatter them about the room. While the music plays, the players dance about the room like graceful swans (or ugly ducklings, as the case may be). The moment the music stops players must leap on to a nearby island. Anyone failing to fit both feet on an island has to drop out, taking one of the islands with them. The last player left playing the game is the winner. Any players who appear to be hovering near an island when they should be gliding about face immediate disqualification.

Musical Rush

In order to play this game you will need several small objects, one fewer than there are players.

Place these small objects – pencils, coins, buttons, corks and the like – in the middle of the room and get the players to form a loose circle around the objects but at least two metres away from them. While the music plays, the players must dance around the circle in time to it. As soon as it stops, they must all rush forward and pick up an object. One player will fail to find an object and he must drop out, taking one object with him. The last player left dancing is the winner.

Musical Scramble

This is a twist on the classic Musical Chairs (page 273). In order to play you will need six or more players and as many chairs as there are players.

The chairs are placed in a circle, the seats facing outwards. The players stand in front of their chairs until the music starts, when they all begin dancing round the circle in time to the music. As soon as the music stops, the players must all scramble back to their own chairs – the chairs they were standing by before the music started – and sit on them. The last player to get back to his seat each time the music stops is obliged to sit on it for the rest of the game; and he must not be tempted to trip up any of the other players as they dance past! The last player left dancing is the winner.

Musical Stick

The players form a circle and one is given a stick. When the music begins, the player with the stick taps it on the floor three times and passes it on to the person next to him, who also taps it on the floor three times before passing it on. Any player caught with the stick in their hand when the music stops drops out. The last player left in is the winner.

Pandora's Box

Fill a hamper with an eccentric collection of objects – the more eccentric, the better: ear plugs, one left sock, a poker, a pineapple, a champagne cork, a cracker, a marble, a penknife, a toupee, a teddy bear, a love letter, a garlic press, an eye-patch, a knitting needle . . . you get the idea. Basically anything and everything you can grab from around the house.

(*Saethryd says*: Because who doesn't have those sorts of things just lying around the living room? A pineapple, an eye-patch and a toupee? Good grief!)

Once you've done that, also throw in some cards bearing the names of a few of the people who will be playing the game.

Everybody gathers round the hamper and each player, in turn, with eyes closed, picks three objects and two cards. They then have to tell a short story involving all of the objects and the guests named on the cards. The more surreal the objects, the more surreal the story. The player whose tale is judged the most intriguing/hilarious/spooky/engaging is the winner.

Gyles says: In Greek mythology, Pandora was the first human woman created by the deities and the original Pandora's box was actually a jar that contained all the evils of the world. But do not let that trouble you. This is a very engaging game and well worth the effort of the preparation involved.

Play Time

This game is Pandora's Box (page 343) taken to the next level.
You will need at least eight players, six pairs of identical objects, two rooms and oodles of creativity and dramatic nous. The host must prepare, in advance, two or three identical bundles of half a dozen or more assorted items: a doll, a rolling pin, a boiled egg, a whip, a menu, a torch, a cheese-grater; you get the idea.

Divide your guests/children/family/the neighbour who happened to pop round for a coffee and a HobNob into two or three teams and give each team one of the bundles, *without* divulging its contents. Send the teams into different rooms and tell them each to prepare a short play, involving every member of the team and all the props provided in the bundle. Give them ten minutes in which to script and rehearse their productions and then have each team present its drama to the other team. It's fascinating to see how different the plays can be.

Proverbial Pantomime

This is the game in which the Marcel Marceaus of the suburbs can have their day. (Or should that be 'the Marcel Marceaux of the suburbs'?)

Rory says: Who's Marcel Marceau?? Seriously, I have no idea what you are talking about.

Gyles says: Marcel Marceau (1923–2007) was a world-famous French mime artist, silent but brilliant. In 1957, when he came to London, I saw him playing Bip the Clown and thought he was wonderful. He was a national hero in France and when he died, on French radio they had two minutes of noise in his honour.

To play Proverbial Pantomime players are divided into two teams and everyone writes down a reasonably well-known proverb or maxim on a scrap of paper. Here are some handy proverbs that work well with the game.

A rolling stone gathers no moss.
Look before you leap.
A bird in the hand is worth two in the bush.
Too many cooks spoil the broth.

Many hands make light work.

A stitch in time saves nine.

Don't put all your eggs in one basket.

People who live in glass houses should undress in the basement.

The two teams then exchange proverbs and the first player in the first team is required to get up and act out, in mime, the proverb he has been given. His team-mates must guess the proverb from his performance and if they can do so, the team gains a point.

Teams may not put any questions to the player performing the mime. They are only allowed one guess and one minute for their deliberations. They are allowed to ask him to repeat his mime *once* if they are unable to agree on the proverb without an encore. If, then, they still can't agree, the members of the opposing team (excepting the player who wrote down the proverb in question) can have a go at guessing.

The players take it in turn to act out their proverbs and the team with the most points at the end wins. As their prize, the victors are allowed thirty seconds in which to blow the proverbial raspberries at the vanquished. This is the best part of the game.

Dumb Nursery Rhymes

For people who love miming, here's a variation on the game above. The players divide into small groups or three or four, and one group at a time leaves the room to choose a nursery rhyme and to work out how they should act it. When they have decided, they come back and perform to the others. They can use any props they like but they can only act with dumb-show. Anyone caught talking has to leave the stage.

The Railway Carriage Game

This game is great to play with a gang. Two of you play at a time and the rest make up the audience.

The two players leave the room while the members of the audience choose a separate phrase or sentence for each of them. The phrases can be as simple and as ridiculous as the audience likes – anything from 'God Save the Queen!' to 'I've got a lovely bunch of coconuts!' will do. Once the phrases have been chosen, the players are summoned back to the room individually and each is given their own phrase. They are not told what their opponent's phrase is.

When the two players have been given their phrases, in front of the audience, they climb into an imaginary railway carriage where they conduct a conversation for the length of a five-minute journey. During the conversation they can say whatever they like to each other, but at some point they must manage to slip their given phrase into the conversation and they must attempt to do so as discreetly and naturally as possible.

When five minutes are up, the first player has to guess what the second player's phrase is and the second player has to guess what the first player's is.

Gyles says: This game has a rich and illustrious history. Not only did it enjoy a couple of seasons as a prime-time television game show in the 1980s, hosted by a presenter of truly remarkable ability and charisma, it was also played at British Spy Schools throughout the First and Second World Wars (which we won). Enough said.

'What are we shouting?'

Players divide into two teams and the first team goes away into a corner and thinks of a well-known phrase or proverb. Let's suppose it's 'A stitch in time saves nine'. If there are six members of the team, each member is given a different word to shout. If there are more than six, then some members will have to shout the same word. When they have chosen the phrase and sorted out who is going to shout which word, they go over to the other team and, on the word 'Go!', shout their words all together. The other team can ask to hear the words shouted three times before it tries to guess what the proverb or phrase is. If it fails to guess correctly, the first team can go back to their corner, choose another phrase or proverb and have another go. However, if the team that's listening can guess what the phrase or proverb is, it's their turn to go into a corner and think of a phrase of their own.

Here are some good phrases to shout:

Any old iron! (for three players)
God save the Queen! (for four players)
Hark! the Herald Angels sing (for five players)
Too many cooks spoil the broth (for six players)
Little Jack Horner sat in the corner (for seven players)

Country HOUSE Weekend

The grand country house weekend is one of our finest British traditions, and they go barmy for these games at Balmoral, Sandringham and, on a wet Wednesday, even at Kensington Palace, so we're told.

Of course, we don't all have a country estate that we can nip off to on the weekends, but lots of us do have large groups of friends who love hanging out together, holidaying together and spending the weekend together. Many of the games in this section benefit from being played in big groups, so they also benefit from having big houses or spaces to play them in. Others are longer games perfect to linger over when you have more time to relax and enjoy each other's company.

This is the only chapter in which we have included outdoor games. We thought we simply couldn't give you the ingredients for the perfect playful weekend away without including a few outdoor pursuits. In fact, most of the outdoor games can be easily adapted to be played inside.

On page 404 you will find our House Party Mix. Played after a large dinner or drinks party, it is a fun way to add some structure to an evening of otherwise inconsequential merriment and so mark out the occasion as something a bit special. So whether it be at Downton Abbey or in downtown Manchester, get ready for a weekend of rich, rewarding and (who knows?) even ribald recreation.

All Change

This is a fabulous ice-breaker if you have game guests.

Since people tend to hide behind their clothes, the best way to get to know your fellow guests is to try theirs on for size. As people arrive at the start of the weekend or evening, the men and the boys are sent off to one room and the girls and the women to another. When they are there they all swap clothes and spend the rest of the day or evening in each other's outfits, freed from their own protective clothing and enchanted by the eccentricity of their own behaviour.

If you want to get really eccentric, you can have the men and the women swap clothes . . . but we'll leave that to your discretion.

Ankles

Ankles is a glorious game to play with a large gathering. It is wonderfully silly.

Players divide into two teams. One team is sent from the room while members of the other team take off their shoes and socks/stockings/tights and lie side by side, where they are covered top to toe in a heavy sheet, duvet or blanket. Only their feet and ankles must be visible.

The outsiders then return to the room and examine the feet on display, handling them as necessary, while not descending to the cheap trick of tickling soles in the hope of securing an identifiable giggle. The outsiders each make a list of names of the bodies to which they sense the different feet belong, and the outsider most successful in matching ankle to individual is the winner. The roles are then reversed.

It is a kindness to forewarn the guests that the game will be played, so that they can come to the party with feet prepared for close inspection and some of the crafty guys can even arrive with toes carefully camouflaged with nail varnish. Also, with fair warning, those with podophobia can decide to stay at home.

Balloon Battle

For this game each player will need a rolled-up newspaper, a balloon and a piece of string.

Players blow up their balloons and tie them to their ankles. Once this is done, battle can commence. What happens is this. While attempting to protect his own balloon, each player tries to burst as many of the other balloons as possible, using only his rolled-up newspaper. No balloon may be touched by hand. A player whose balloon is burst is eliminated, and the last player left in is the winner.

Bluffo

Bluffo is loosely based on the classic television panel game, *Call My Bluff*. Or was *Call My Bluff* inspired by Bluffo? Cultural historians (and intellectual property lawyers) are still discussing the issue.

To play Bluffo the players divide into two teams and huddle in separate corners to work out who is going to do what. The host has previously provided each team with a series of categories – such as Plays, American Soap Operas, Dangerous Sports, Flowers – depending on the particular interests of the players. If team A has four members and the first category is Plays, then each member will have to tell the members of team B about a particular play. Three of the plays described by the members of team A will not exist. The description of the plays – the details of the casts and celebrated productions – will all have been invented by the team. Only one play described will be a real one, and team B must detect it. If team B guesses the true play, they gain a point. If they pick one of the bluffs, team A gains a point.

Teams take it in turns to present their true and false information and the team that is more successful in spotting the truth in their opponents and concealing it from them themselves will have the most points and will win.

(Does this sound a little like *Would I Lie to You?* Now where did they get that idea from?)

Gyles says: The TV show *Call My Bluff* was devised by a pair of remarkable Americans, Bill Todman and Mark Goodson – the Simon Cowells of their day – who made millions in dollars, pounds and yen packaging parlour games for the small screen. *What's My Line?* was one of their biggest international successes. In the 1970s I tried to emulate them in the UK, but got no further than creating *Vintage Quiz* for ITV and *The Railway Carriage Game* for the BBC. Neither show sold abroad, though there was *talk* of Finland taking up an option on *The Railway Carriage Game*.

Find the Leader

This is a great game to play with the whole family, from the little ones up.

One player leaves the room. Everyone else sits in a circle on the floor and chooses a leader. The leader then performs a series of simple movements, such as clapping his hands or patting his head or shaking his fists in the air. The other players have to copy the leader's movements and change theirs exactly as he does.

The player who left the room is now brought back and stands in the middle of the circle. He must try to discover which of the players sitting in the circle is the leader. Obviously, the leader will try not to change movements when the player in the middle is looking at him, but if the player in the middle has an eagle eye then he should be able to catch the leader quite quickly. Once caught, the leader leaves the room, the player in the middle joins the circle and a new leader is chosen.

Find the Proverb

This is a game that needs some preparation. It's fun to play before dinner on a Saturday night, or when people first arrive as a bit of an ice-breaker.

You will want as many proverbs as there are going to be players. Once you have chosen the proverbs, divide each one into three parts and write one part on each of three cards. For example:

Card 1	Card 2	Card 3
Too many	cooks	spoil the broth
Many hands	make light	work
A stitch	in time	saves nine
A bird in the hand	is worth two	in the bush
A rolling	stone gathers	no moss

Before the players arrive, hide *two* cards of each proverb somewhere around the house. At the beginning of the game, give each player one of the remaining cards. The player then has to work out what their proverb is and has to set about finding the other two cards to complete it. Players should work alone and may not talk while they are looking for their cards. The first person to complete their proverb wins. The last person to complete theirs has to pay a forfeit.

Front and Back Race

For this game you will need an even number of players, two saucers and a selection of small objects for each team.

The players divide into two teams and stand sideways, in line, facing each other. On the ground at the head of each team are two saucers, one of which is empty, the other of which is filled with a dozen or so small objects, such as a coin, a rubber, a button, a pencil, a potato, and so on.

On the word 'Go!' the leader of each team picks up the first item and passes it to the second person in the line, who passes it to the third, who passes it to the fourth, and so on down the line. When the object reaches the last player, she begins to pass it back down the line again but this time *behind her back*. When the leader receives the objects behind his back, he places them in the empty saucer. The first team to have transferred all its objects from one saucer to the other has won.

To make the game as much fun as possible, there should be at *least* twice as many objects in the saucer as there are players in each team so that at some point in the race every player is passing objects both forward and back, in front and behind.

The Hat Game

The Hat Game, sometimes called Celebrity, is a country weekend classic.

At the start of the game all the players are given a pencil and five pieces of paper. On each piece of paper they must write the name of a well-known figure – be it a celebrity, sports personality, politician, musician, author, artist, cartoon character or fictional character. The only essential is that it must be someone that you can have a realistic expectation that most people will have heard of.

Once the names are written down, the pieces of paper are folded and put in a hat, where they are given a good mix-up. Players then split into teams, with a minimum of two teams but as many as is appropriate for the amount of people present. (Boys versus girls, though predictable, usually proves a fun split.)

The first player pulls a name out of the hat and tries to get his team to guess as quickly as possible the person he or she is describing. The player must not name the personality, but other clear clues are allowed. So, for example, if a player pulled Barack Obama from the hat, they could say 'Current President of the United States'. The player has one minute in which to pull as many names out of the hat as possible. When his team guesses correctly, the piece of paper is put to one side and the team score a point. If the team fail to identify the person named, or if the person describing decides to pass on that particular name, it goes back in the hat.

The teams take it in turns to play, and each player in a team takes their turn to be the player pulling names out of the hat.

Once all the names have been guessed and the scores have been tallied, it's on to round two.

All the names go back in the hat and round two is played in exactly the same way as round one *except* that this time players may only use one word to describe the person named on the piece of paper. This works because by this point everyone knows what all the names are, so if you were to say simply the word 'President' your team-mates would quickly guess 'Barack Obama'.

But the game isn't over yet. At the end of round two, the scores for that round are added to the scores for the first round, and the names go back into the hat for the final time. In round three, you may not say anything when you pull the name from the hat: it is essentially a round of Charades. We shall leave it up to you to think of a suitable mime for Barack . . . Gyles usually mimes bounding up the steps to the presidential helicopter; Saethryd stands still with her right hand placed on her heart, offering a solemn presidential salute; Rory tries to hum the 'Star-Spangled Banner', but that's not really allowed.

This game is lots of fun and, depending on the number of players, can take up much of the afternoon or evening, which makes it good for a wet country afternoon or for after a hearty country dinner.

Hide and Seek

Hide and Seek is one of those games we all seem to learn by osmosis. Most people can't remember a time when they didn't know how to play it. It is often one of the first games we teach our own children. While it is very much part of our childhoods, intriguingly, it is just as much fun to play once you're grown-up. Just in case you don't know them, or need reminding, here are the rules.

A particular spot is chosen as 'home'. The Seeker stands there, covers his eyes and counts up to fifty while the other players scatter and hide themselves in various parts of the house. When he has counted to fifty, the Seeker calls out 'Coming, ready or not!' and goes off in search of the other players. The last player to be found by the Seeker becomes the Seeker for the next round.

There are other variations.

Rather than remaining hidden away under the bed, behind the curtain or in the laundry basket, players move round the house with ninja-like stealth and foxlike cunning in order to try to reach the home spot without being seen by the Seeker. If a player is spotted by the Seeker, they are out. If a player manages to make it back to home without being spotted, he calls out '*Alle alle auch sind frie*' (German for 'Everyone, everyone is also free') and the rest of the players can return safely to home base.

In a version sometimes called Chain Hide and Seek, when the Seeker finds a player, they hold hands and go seeking for the others together.

When they find the next player, that player joins the chain, and so on, until everyone is found. This is a fun way to play when you have a large group or small children, as it keeps everyone involved.

A spooky version, good to play on Hallowe'en after a getting-to-know-you round of Ghosts (page 448), involves turning off all the lights and having the Seeker search with only a torch. When he catches a player in the beam, that player is given the torch and becomes the Seeker.

Light and Shade

In the days when people kept roaring fires in their drawing rooms, this was a very popular game. Nowadays it's all central heating and sitting rooms, but if you are lucky enough to be staying in a massive country pile with an equally large inglenook, then this is the game for you. If not, a bright electric lamp works just as well.

To prepare for the game, a white sheet is hung across the room and a light is shone on to it. The players then divide into two teams and the members of one team take it in turn to walk across the room behind the sheet so that their shadows are thrown on to it. The opposing team sits out front guessing who it is who is going by. Obviously, the shadow players must do all they can to disguise their silhouettes. After each member of the first team has crossed the room at least twice the teams swap round.

At the end of the game, the team with the most correct guesses wins.

Mafia

Mafia is a game of skill and strategy, deduction and deception. Also known as Werewolf, it became immensely popular in Britain in the 1990s but it is actually a Russian game that originated from the psychology department of Moscow State University in the mid 1980s and has been played on campuses and in student digs around the world ever since. It bears a resemblance to Wink Murder (page 306), but has added elements that make it more absorbing. Different versions of Mafia have evolved over the years. Here we present the simplest.

When the players or guests arrive, or before the game is about to start, everyone playing must pick a folded piece of paper from a hat. These will have been prepared by the host, who does not play the game (or at least the first round) but instead acts as games master.

The majority of the pieces of paper will be blank, but a certain number with have the letter M written on them. If you pick a piece of paper marked with an M, you are one of the Mafia. If you have picked a blank piece of paper, you are one of the townsfolk.

It is important at this stage that no one reveals their identity.

When play is about to commence the games master gathers everyone together, where they can all see each other. (Note: This game works very well at a dinner table.) He or she then declares that night has fallen, and that all the players must close their eyes. When 'night' falls all the members of the Mafia open their eyes and silently acknowledge each other. It is very important not to give the game away by getting the giggles or giving any indication of who you may be.

Through pointing, nodding and other such gestures, the Mafia must choose a victim from the innocent townsfolk who still sit with their eyes closed. Once a unanimous decision has been made, the Mafia all nod their heads in agreement and close their eyes. The games master now declares that it is daybreak and *all* the players can open their eyes.

The games master announces which player met with a grisly death during the night. Everyone then debates about who at the table is a member of the Mafia. Obviously those who are in the Mafia will know who their fellow accomplices are, so they will be required to lie, deceive and cast doubt over the innocent. Those who are innocent will need to work out who is lying, who is telling the truth and who are in cahoots with each other.

At any point a player may accuse another player of being in the Mafia. (An actual member of the Mafia may even accuse an innocent to throw the rest of the players off his scent.) When this happens the group has to vote on whether or not they believe the accusation; if more than half those gathered vote to support the accusation the accused player is 'lynched'; this means they are eliminated from the game and their actual allegiance is revealed.

After a 'lynching' the games master will declare that night has fallen once more, and the process will begin again. The Mafia will choose another player to be murdered and another round of daytime accusations, denials and lynchings will occur.

The game ends when all the mafia have been correctly lynched or all the innocent townsfolk have been murdered or falsely accused.

Saethryd says: This is a fantastic game. My favourite moment is when the Mafia all silently open their eyes and know they are in cahoots! For maximum enjoyment, think carefully about the proportion of Mafia to innocents. You can have anywhere from two upwards, but we find the game works best with at least three and up to about a third of your guests.

In more advance versions of Mafia players are given a number of different roles, the most common of which is Detective, but there is also Mayor, Barman, Doctor, Witness – a whole village's worth.

If you would like to know some of the different roles and variations, get in touch via the *Lost Art of Having Fun* Facebook page or Twitter, and we will let you know a few of our favourites.

Murder in the Dark

Murder in the Dark is a chilling game that's definitely not for those with weak hearts and sensitive dispositions.

To prepare, as many slips of paper as there are players are put into a bowl. All but two are blank. On one there is a circle; on another a cross. The slips of paper are folded so no one can see which is which. Each player picks a slip of paper from the bowl at random. The player who picks the circle is the detective and he identifies himself. The player who picks the cross is the murderer and says nothing.

All the lights in the house are turned off, and all the players, apart from the detective, disperse throughout the house. The murderer, his black heart beating faster and faster, prowls through the gloom until he chances upon a suitable victim in a lonely spot. Creeping up on his victim, the murderer seizes the poor wretch – by the hand, by the leg, perhaps not by the neck! – and whispers in his ear 'You're dead'. The victim screams frenziedly, and falls to the floor as the murderer slinks away.

As soon as the scream is heard, the other players must remain where they are, while the detective makes his way as quickly as possible to the scene of the crime, switching on all the lights on his way.

The detective inspects the scene of the crime, notes the whereabouts of all the suspects and summons everyone into the drawing room to be questioned in true Agatha Christie fashion. By questioning the suspects as to their movements and their location at the time of the murder, and by looking for inconsistencies in their stories, as well as by watching for signs of guilt in their faces, the detective has to identify the murderer.

Each player must answer all the detective's questions with the truth and nothing but the truth – except, of course, for the murderer, who can lie as much as he likes until asked the direct question 'Are you the murderer?', when he must break down and confess all.

The detective is allowed two guesses at the identity of the murderer. If he fails to nail his man, the murderer has got away with murder . . . and wins the game.

Newspaper Quiz

This is a game for two teams and a question-master. It is ideal to play over a lazy Sunday breakfast. The teams don't need to be very big: in fact the game works best of all when there are only two or three players in each team.

To begin, give both teams a copy of the same newspaper and allow them five minutes in which to study it. When the teams have had a chance to look through their papers, the question-master asks a series of questions about different topics — the answers to all of which can be found in the newspapers. The first team to come up with the correct answer wins a point.

At the end of ten (or twenty) questions, the team with the most points has won.

Pan Tapping

Afirm favourite of the Queen's sister, the late Princess Margaret, this is a classic that no doubt is still being played by Kate, Wills and Harry on wet weekends at Kensington Palace, where the Cambridges are bringing up wee George in the very apartment where Princess Margaret used to play the game. Here's what happens.

One player is sent from the room (probably to the bathroom, where he will nose through your bathroom cabinet, but never mind), while the others decide on something they want him to do on his return: peel a grape, perhaps; or switch on the television; or kiss the woman everyone knows he has been wanting to kiss for years.

When the player is brought back into the room, another player guides his actions by beating on the bottom of a saucepan with a metal spoon. (If you are not playing the game in a palace or a castle, a non-stick frying pan and a wooden spoon might be kinder on the neighbours.) When the outsider moves towards the object he is to touch, say the woman he must kiss, the pan-tapper loudly beats his instrument. When he moves away from the object, the pan-tapper beats more softly. The nearer the outsider comes to the object, the louder the beating becomes, till the outsider has done what he had to do.

Post-it Note Game

A lso known as the Rizla Game, this student classic is a great getting-to-know-you game or an entertaining way to pass some time after dinner.

If you are playing the game to encourage mixing, greet your guests as they arrive with a stack of Post-it notes and a pen in hand. Write the name of a well-known figure, alive or dead, real or fictional, on the Post-it note and stick it to the person's forehead. Then send them in to mingle. The idea of the game is to discover who you are – in other words, the name attached to your forehead. Players can ask fellow guests questions requiring 'Yes' or 'No' answers in order to work out their mystery identity.

If you are playing the game seated in a group, get everyone to write a name on a Post-it note or Rizla paper and stick it to the forehead of the person sitting next to them.

The first person to guess their own identity is the winner, the last one to do is the loser and must perform a forfeit.

Royal Academy

This game is probably even older than the Royal Academy of Arts, which was founded in 1768. It has even been said that the game has produced more exciting artwork than ever was seen at a Royal Academy Summer Exhibition. Whatever the age and merits of the game or the Academy, this exercise is ideal for reviving flagging guests over pre-dinner G and Ts.

The players divide into two teams and each team stands or sits around a table or drawing-board at different ends of the room. On the word 'Go!' the leader of each team rushes to the host, who is sitting in the middle of the room and who (in a whisper) gives them both the same subject for a drawing. It could be something simple like 'Snow White and the Seven Dwarfs' or 'An elephant and a giraffe go skiing', or it could be something subtly esoteric such as 'God sitting on a pillow of love' or 'England being engulfed by a wave of emotion'.

Equipped with their subjects, the team leaders run back to their colleagues and begin to draw the given scene. The artist's team-mates make guesses as to what he is drawing, to which he can only reply by nodding or shaking his head. He may draw anything he feels will help his friends, but he may not write any words, and as soon as a correct guess is made – and the players mustn't blurt out their ideas in stentorian tones or their opponents will overhear them – another member of the team darts off to the host to be given a fresh subject.

The first team to have drawn and guessed all the scenes first has won.

Variation

If you would rather, you can play one team at a time, with the teams taking turns and drawing different subjects. This takes a little longer but allows everyone to laugh and cheer and jeer along with the person who is drawing.

Sardines

Queen Victoria played this game. So did most of her subjects. It is one of the most popular parlour games the world has known, and anyone who hasn't played it can't be said to have 'lived' in the full sense of the word.

Sardines is best played in a large house with lots of possible hiding-places. Osborne House on the Isle of Wight is ideal, but, in our experience, the game works in a basement flat in Shepherd's Bush almost as well.

All the players assemble in one room. The first player leaves the room and hides himself away somewhere in the house. The remaining players follow after, one at a time, at one-minute intervals. The second player has to find the first player's hiding-place and join him there. The third player has to find the first two and join them. The fourth player, ditto . . . and so on. The game ends when all the players are packed together – like sardines – in the larder or under the bed or wherever the hiding-place happens to be.

Sardines can also be played as a couples game. Everyone gathers in the designated room and remains there for two or three minutes while a selected couple go forth quietly to hide themselves together somewhere – *anywhere* – in the house. At the end of the two or three minutes, the other guests set out in pairs to search for the hidden couple, and the first pair to locate them in their hideaway must join them there. As each succeeding pair discovers the hideaway, they too must join the occupants . . . silently.

If twenty-six students from the City of London College can perch together on top of a pillar box in Finsbury Circus, Sardines players should have little difficulty packing themselves into roomy downstairs loos and walk-in wardrobes!

Uncle Joshua

This old American game is perfect for playing while warming up round the fire after a bracing afternoon walk through the countryside. The game is based around the verse of an old song:

My Uncle Joshua died last night.
That's too bad; how did he die?
With one eye shut and his mouth awry,
One foot held high and waving goodbye.

The players sit in a circle and the leader begins by saying to player number two 'My Uncle Joshua died last night'. Player number two replies 'That's too bad; how did he die?' 'With one eye shut,' says the leader, closing one eye as he says it. The leader will now keep his eye shut until the end of the game.

It is now player number two's turn and he turns to player number three and says 'My Uncle Joshua died last night', gets the reply 'That's too bad; how did he die?' and answers 'With one eye shut', at which point he too closes his eye, whereupon it becomes player number three's turn.

This goes round the group until all the players are sitting there with one eye shut and it is the leader's turn again. This time he says to player number two 'My Uncle Joshua died last night'. Player number two again replies, 'That's too bad, how did he die?', but this time gets the answer 'With one eye shut and his mouth awry.' At this point the leader screws up his mouth and keeps it screwed up for the rest of the game, while it becomes player number two's turn.

And so it goes on around the group, with the effect that after four full rounds all the players are sitting in the circle with one eye shut, their faces awry, one foot held high and waving goodbye. Any player who gives the wrong answer or is caught opening his eye or failing to wave goodbye drops out. With a bit of luck, nobody will drop out and all the players will end up as winners.

Winking

This is a game for a very large group, preferably sixteen or more players. You will need chairs for half the players and a room large enough to put the chairs in an inward-facing circle.

Place a girl in each chair, except for one chair, which is left empty. Behind each chair, including the empty one, stands a man with his hands resting lightly on the back of the chair, though not touching the girl who is in the chair.

The man standing behind the empty chair begins the game by winking at any one of the girls in any of the other chairs. The girl who is winked at must attempt to get out of her chair and rush to sit in his. The man standing behind the winked-at girl must do his best to stop her. If he manages to get his hands on to her shoulders before she can get away, she has to stay where she is. He replaces his hands on the back of her chair and the man with the empty chair has to wink at another girl in the hope of luring her to his empty chair. However, if the girl who has been winked at does manage to get to the empty chair, it becomes the turn of the man standing behind the newly emptied chair to wink at another girl and get her over to his chair.

At Brandreth Towers, all games are equal opportunities games, so once all the girls have been winked at, the players should change places and the men should sit in all but one of the chairs and the girls should do the winking.

Yes and No

This is another excellent game for getting people to talk to each other at parties. Each player is given five coins (or if you are short of change or worried about the honesty of the players, you can use used matches instead). The players then have to pair off and engage each other in conversation.

The aim of the game is for a player to trick the other player into using the words 'Yes' or 'No'. The first player of the pair to say 'Yes' or 'No' is presented with a penny by the other player. The two players then split up and move on to new partners.

The first player to get rid of his five coins is the winner.

Zoo Quest

In order to play this game you will need a large group of people and a box of chocolates.

Players are split into teams, with three, four or five players in each team. One member of each team is chosen to be the leader and the other players assume the identities of various animals. They should be discouraged from being obvious animals like dogs, cats and cows; instead they should be urged (or coerced) into being, for example, a coyote, a rhinoceros, a hyena, a gorilla, a three-toed sloth, and so forth.

The chocolates are scattered in various locations about the house. The team members then go off in search of the chocolates, leaving their leaders to have a few moments of rest. When a player finds a chocolate, he makes a noise appropriate to the animal he is impersonating, and the leader, on hearing one of his animals, goes and collects the chocolate.

After ten minutes, the team whose leader has collected the most chocolates is the winning team.

Greedy players who eat the chocolates they find instead of calling their leader will be on the losing team, and rightly so . . .

Rory says: I love losing at this game!

IF THE RAIN EVER STOPS . . .

• • •

The idea of outdoor fun and games at weekend country retreats always brings to mind images of the Kennedys – blonde, tanned and glamorous – playing touch football on the lawns of Camelot before retiring for a strong Martini and some political hobnobbing. In real life, in the United Kingdom at least, outdoor fun and games tend to consist more of a quick kick-around before the clouds roll in, the heavens open and everyone's back inside for a strong cup of tea and an actual HobNob.
If the weather does, however, decide to be kind, this selection of group games will enhance any weekend gathering.
Quick, get out there while you still have the chance . . .

Boat Race

The players divide into equal teams.

In each team, one player acts as 'cox' and the rest form the boat.

The players take up squatting positions one behind the other with their hands on the shoulders of the player in front.

On the command 'Go!' the players hop forward as best they can and race over a short course. If a player falls over or lets go of the player in front of him, the ship is sunk. The cox stands in front of his boat calling out the rhythm to help his boat hop along in unison.

The first boat past the finishing line wins.

British Bulldogs

Enjoyed in school playgrounds for the best part of last century, British Bulldogs is a rough and tumble game for the sharp of elbows, not the faint of heart. It is best played on a large lawn or a surface where hitting the ground isn't going to hurt too much.

The rules of the game are simple. Everyone gathers at one end of the lawn. Apart from the Bulldog, who stands in the middle.

On the command 'Go!' the players must try to get to safety on the other side of lawn, and the Bulldog has to stop them. If the Bulldog touches you in any way you're caught. When a player is caught he becomes another Bulldog.

The winner is the last player to be caught.

Cage the Bear

One player is chosen to be the bear and the other players are the hunters. The hunters form a circle round the bear. They stand at arm's length from the bear with their hands joined and move slowly, circling round him. The aim of the game is for the bear to try and break free.

The hunters must keep their hands joined and they must not hold on to the bear. They can move their arms up and down to try and block his way. When the bear escapes or the hunters break the rules, a new bear is chosen.

Lions

Saethryd says: This game comes courtesy of an old friend of mine, who very kindly used to take me on posh country house weekends where it was all dressing for dinner, clay-pigeon shooting, passive-aggressive croquet and, of course, games. As kindly as ever, he can still be bothered to remind me of the rules of one of my favourites twenty years on. Take it away, Will . . .

This game is best played with six to twelve people. It can be played indoors in a house with at least two staircases, or outdoors in a big garden that goes all the way round the house. If playing at night, one can dim the lights for added tension.

One person is selected (or selects themselves) as the lion. Everyone else is a sheep. The game starts with the lion counting to twenty and the sheep spreading themselves about. The sheep should note that this isn't hide and seek, and they need to be mobile. So it is better to lurk behind a door than to hide under a bed.

Once the count is over, the lion shouts 'Coming!' and starts to hunt his prey. The sheep are caught by sight. When he sees one, the lion must identify them by name – that is, he can't simply say 'Saw you!' When caught, the sheep have to stand still exactly where they were when the lion called their name. They are not allowed to move.

Caught sheep can be rescued by being touched by free sheep. Caught sheep are only allowed to say one word: 'Rescue'. Therefore they have to be exceedingly cunning and use intonation/tone of voice to communicate their real wishes to their fellow sheep. For example, if the lion is nearby, they don't actually want to be rescued, since those attempting to free them will themselves be caught. In this situation, they should say 'R-r-r-r-rescue' (with an affected stammer). This will communicate to their fellow sheep the lion's whereabouts. When caught sheep are certain the lion is elsewhere, they should shout 'Rescue, rescue' in an agitated voice, thereby communicating to their fellow sheep that the coast is clear.

The game continues until either all the sheep are caught at the same time, in which case the lion wins, or the lion gives up, in which case the sheep have collectively won.

Note: If there are a large number of sheep or, for example, young children are the lion, the game can be played with two lions.

Variation

The game can be played in a single (ideally fairly large) room in total (or very near total) darkness. Then the lion has to catch the sheep by touching them (when he does so, he should call out 'Caught you!', to identify himself as the lion). Otherwise the game proceeds along the same lines.

Queenie

This is another old favourite that's an ideal game to play if you've got lots of players and a very large field.

One player is chosen to be Queenie and she stands at one end of the field holding a ball with her back to all the other players. At the command 'Go!' Queenie throws the ball over her shoulder and counts to five while the other players all scramble furiously for it.

When Queenie reaches 'Five' she shouts 'Stop!' and everyone must stand completely still with their hands behind their backs. Queenie now turns around and has to guess which of the players has managed to get hold of the ball. If she guesses correctly, the person who got the ball becomes Queenie for the next round. But if she picks someone who doesn't have the ball, she has another round as Queenie, turns her back on the others players again and throws the ball over her shoulder once more.

Scavenger Hunt

No weekend in the country in complete without a long walk. Unfortunately we have found that the kids tend to get bored after about ten minutes. Never fear! You can keep them entertained by devising a country walk scavenger hunt: they'll be so busy trying to complete their collection, they won't notice the miles slip by.

The idea is very simple: before you head out give everyone a list of between ten and twenty items they need to collect. The first one to collect all the items is the winner. Adapt your list to the season and location. Here are some suggestions of items that you could include:

1. A conker
2. An oak leaf
3. An acorn
4. A dock leaf
5. A twig
6. A smooth pebble
7. A flower of some sort
8. Some moss
9. A blackberry
10. A piece of bark
11. A fir-cone
12. A yellow flower of some sort

13. Some hay
14. An ear of corn
15. A sycamore leaf
16. A leaf from a birch tree
17. A thorn
18. A pine-needle
19. A pink flower of some sort
20. A four-leafed clover (or, if you are not that lucky, a three-leafed clover will do instead)

Scrum

There's nothing posh folk like more than a good game of rugger, what ho! Even if you didn't go to public school, have thighs like tree-trunks or ears like cauliflowers you can still enjoy rugby. Here's our more egalitarian version.

Two teams are formed and they confront each other, heads down, in a rugger scrum formation, across a line drawn on the grass. The aim of the game is to cross the line, so the two teams indulge in a battle of strengths in an attempt to move forward. The first team to cross the line has won. Then it's back-slapping, beer-drinking and communal baths for all.

Sheepdog Trials

For this game you will need an even number of players, blindfolds for half the players, and various obstacles to place around the garden.

The object of the game is for one player – the shepherd – to guide another player who is blindfolded – the sheepdog – round a series of obstacles and into a pen by giving verbal instructions only.

The pairs set off one at a time and their journey round the course is timed. The fastest pair wins the prize.

The dogs, of course, must be blindfolded before the obstacles are set up. They are then led to the starting line and the dog must obey the shepherd's instructions in every detail. For example, if the shepherd says 'Three steps forward, turn sharp right, now four steps forward, now a little to the left, now four steps forward', then that is exactly what the dog must do, even if it leads him straight into a hedge.

Once all the dogs have been round the course and a winner has been declared, the dogs become the shepherds, the shepherds become the dogs, the obstacles are altered and the game begins all over again.

Rory says: I love this game.

Slapjack

All the players stand in a circle facing inwards with their hands behind their backs. One player is chosen as 'Jack', and Jack moves out of the circle and runs round the back of the other players, slapping the hands of one of them as he passes. He then keeps on running round the circle. The player whose hand Jack has just slapped must now leave his place in the circle and run round the outside of the circle in the opposite direction to Jack and must attempt to get back to his original place before Jack gets there. If Jack gets to the slapped player's place first, the slapped player becomes Jack for the next round. If the slapped player beats Jack back to their place, then Jack has to stay as Jack for the next round.

Tag

The game of Tag comes in several versions, three of which are as follows.

Chain Tag

At the beginning of the game, two players join hands and together they chase the remaining players. Whenever they tag anyone, that player joins hands with them and helps them chase the others. Gradually a chain is built up. The last person to be tagged by the chain is the winner.

French Tag

One player is chosen to be the chaser. He has to chase all the other players and try to touch them on an awkward part of the body, such as the back of the neck or the ankle or the knee. Where the chaser touches the player who is tagged that player must keep a hand on that spot – the back of the neck or the ankle or the knee – until he in turn manages to tag another player.

Hopping Tag

A chaser is chosen who has to tag as many players as he can. As soon as a player has been tagged – that is to say, touched by the chaser – he joins the chaser's side, chases after other players and tags them. The last player left untagged is the winner. The only twist to the game is that the players, whether they are chasing or being chased, can only move about by hopping on one leg. They can change legs as often as they like and when they are standing still they can have both feet firmly planted on the ground. But the moment they move, they must hop.

Triangular Tug of War

This is a splendid game to play if you are in the country and can get hold of a strong piece of rope that is at least eight metres long.

You need three players and you begin by tying the ends of the rope together to form a loop. Each player takes hold of the rope with one hand and the players stand with an equal distance between them in the shape of a triangle. About a metre behind each player there is an object – a ball, a hat, a scarf, a stone, a coat – and the aim of the game is to tug at the rope and pull it towards the object that is right behind you and pick that object up. All three players are tugging in different directions and the first player who succeeds in picking up his object is the winner.

Tug of War/Oranges and Lemons

You will need at least six players for this game to be its most enjoyable.

Two of the players are chosen to form an arch. To do this they stand facing each other, holding hands with their arms raised in the air. One of the players is 'Oranges' and the other is 'Lemons'. The other players march round in a large circle, one behind another continually passing under the arch. As they march they sing this traditional English nursery rhyme:

Oranges and Lemons,
Say the bells of St Clement's.
You owe me five farthings,
Say the bells of St Martin's.
When will you pay me?
Say the bells of Old Bailey.
When I grow rich,
Say the bells of Shoreditch.
Pray, when will that be?
Say the bells of Stepney.
I'm sure I don't know,
Says the great bell at Bow.
Here comes a candle to light you to bed,
Here comes a chopper to chop off your head.

As the last line is sung the players forming the arch move their arms up and down, finally bringing them down to trap one of the players marching through the arch. The game continues in this way until all the players have been trapped under the arch.

As the players are trapped they are asked to choose Oranges or Lemons. They join a line on one side of the arch or the other, according to their choice, each player holding the waist of the player in front.

The game then concludes with a tug of war between the Oranges and the Lemons.

Two Dogs, One Bone

For this game you will need an even number of players, an umpire and something to act as the 'bone'. Traditionally it is a ball, but you can use any appropriate object, or even a real bone if you've brought Fido with you.

The players divide into two teams and the teams sit in two rows facing each other with a gap of at least two metres between the rows. The players are all numbered, starting with number one at the right-hand side of each team. On the ground, midway between the two teams, the 'bone' is placed.

The umpire stands to the side and, when everyone is ready, calls out a number, say 'Three'. Number Three from each team rushes forward towards the bone, tries to grab it and get back to his seat without being touched by his opponent. If he succeeds in doing this, his team scores a point. If he fails, the opposing team scores the point.

A player can't touch his opponent unless the opponent is holding the bone. If both players arrive at the bone at the same time, they don't have to make an immediate grab for it. They can encircle it warily, going in as close as they dare, and can then attempt to snatch it and escape when they get a chance.

After each grab, the bone is returned to its position in the middle. Play goes on for a set period of time and when the time is up the team with the highest score wins.

Gyles says: The Brandreths are dog lovers. Saethryd and Rory have a dog called Crosby, aka the 'Crobster'. Our French poodle was called Fido, but we spelled it 'Phydeaux', of course. For years we had a lovely old mongrel who thought he was called 'Down Boy'.

HOUSE PARTY MIX

* * *

The house party mix is essentially the Country House Weekend Olympics. Guests are split into teams and embark upon a series of games, totting up points as they go, with one team eventually crowned the winner. It works best on a weekend away or an overnight stay, as it takes a bit of time and preparation. It also requires quite a bit of space. Each room in the house is turned into a games 'station' manned by one of the hosts or a helper. The teams set off round the house visiting each station in turn before reconvening in the living room to hear the results.

Over the course of the next few pages we make some suggestions for games that work well in the house party mix, but you could use any combination of many of the games in previous chapters. Kim's Game (page 29), for example, is an excellent game to throw into the house party mix.

It is best to have as many stations as you have teams, so that there is always fun to be had and no teams are left twiddling their thumbs. Stagger the teams so they each start at a different station and have clear directions as to the flow and order of the games. You want games that each take roughly the same amount of time to complete.

The final game (the bonus game) that all the teams will play once they finish their circuit of games should be one that everyone can play together in the living room while waiting for other teams to finish. Advertisements or Who's This? are excellent final games.

Advertisements

This game is a test of observation – and the power of advertising. It relies on the fact that much magazine and newspaper advertising places less emphasis on pictures of the product than on 'images' – sun-drenched beaches, pretty girls, laughing family groups, cartoon characters, and so on.

Some preparation is required beforehand. You need to sort through a number of old magazines and newspapers, cutting out suitable pictures from advertisements for well-known products. The advertisements should be neither too familiar nor too obscure. You will need to cut out of the pictures the name or any other telltale indicator of the product being advertised (for example, the logo). Any number of pictures between twelve and twenty should be sufficient. The pictures must be numbered, and may either be pasted on to a board or simply laid out on a table where all the players can see them.

Each of the teams is given a pencil and paper, and they have ten minutes in which to write down the names of the products being advertised. When it comes to scoring, a team gets 1 point for identifying the type of product being advertised (for example, a watch) and two for the specific brand (for example, Rolex).

Ball in the Bucket
(Flower Pot/Watering Can)

It's not rocket science, this game, nor is it brain surgery. What it is, is surprisingly entertaining.

Waiting in the hallway will be a host or helper with a ball –a tennis, golf or ping-pong ball, even a bean-bag will do – and three oddly shaped receptacles placed at different distances down the hallway. Team members line up to take their turn at throwing the ball into the bucket/flower pot/watering can. You get 1 point for the easiest/closest receptacle, 2 points for the second, 3 for third.

There is a five-minute time limit for each team. At the end of five minutes the team's total points are totted up and they are on their way to the bedroom to see what delights are in store for them there.

Bun Biting

This is a hilarious and messy game best played in the kitchen. You will need string, some soft buns, or if you are feeling particularly mischievous and your guests are wearing clothes they are not too precious about, jam-filled doughnuts.

String up as many buns as there are players in each team. We tie the ends of the string around the handles of two opposing kitchen cabinets and then have the buns dangling down at 30-cm intervals.

The players each line up next to a bun and, on the instruction 'Go!' they have to eat the buns as quickly as possible *without* using their hands.

The time it takes the slowest team member to finish their bun is recorded. When the house party mix scores are being totalled, points are awarded in descending amounts for the fastest of these scores, so if there are six teams it is 6 points for the fastest, 5 for the second fastest, and so on, ending up with 1 point for the slowest.

Guessing Game

P rior to the party, fill different containers with different objects and the teams have to guess how many objects are in each container. Write down each team's guesses, and when you are totting up points at the end, the team that gets the closest gets 2 points and the runners-up get 1 point.

Here are some ideas for containers and things to put in them:

A jam jar full of dried peas   How many peas?

A bottle full of rubber bands   How many rubber bands?

A jar full of wool   How many inches/cm of wool?

A teapot packed with tea bags   How many tea bags?

A plastic bag full of nuts   How many nuts?

SENSORY GAMES

· · ·

Feelers

Fill a pillowcase with assorted odds and ends – a large orange (which could be a grapefruit), a tenpenny piece (which could be a twopenny piece), a back-scratcher (which could be a fork), a yo-yo (which could be anything) – and pass the pillowcase around the players.

Each player may feel it for thirty seconds and then the team confers and writes down a list of the pillowcase's supposed contents. One point is awarded for each correct guess.

For the benefit of the psychics, put a book into the pillowcase as well. Everyone will guess it's a book, but only those with very special gifts will be able to supply the title.

Noises Off

The team gather, pen and paper at the ready, and then the host or helper ducks behind the sofa or under the dining-room table – anywhere where they can't be seen – and makes a series of noises, such as pulling a cork from a bottle, or flicking their fingers, breaking a cream cracker, jangling a bunch of keys, gargling, or brushing a shoe. The team members then confer and write down what they think the noises are. There is 1 point for each correct guess.

For those of you who live in the modern age, you can use your smart phone to record a series of random sounds throughout the day and then play it back to each team. It's a lot more efficient, but perhaps not quite as much fun as hiding behind the sofa with your primary school recorder.

Tastebuds

Fill a number of cups with a variety of different and distinctively flavoured liquids. Blindfold the players, who take it in turns to sniff and sip the assortment of fluids and note their guesses as to what the cups contain.

Water, cold tea, brandy, cough mixture, lemon juice, quinine, diluted washing-up liquid and the like are not difficult to recognise. Telling the difference between cocoa and drinking chocolate, between rainwater and Evian, between Barsac and Sauternes, is rather more demanding and entertaining.

What's the Smell?

Before the party, lay out six saucers on a tray and into each saucer put some sort of substance that has a strong and recognisable smell — cocoa, curry powder, a rose, orange peel, lavender and coffee, for example. Leave the tray in the kitchen or somewhere the players won't see it.

When the time comes to play the game, blindfold all the players. Then bring the tray into the room and place it on the table. The blindfolded players take it in turns to come up to the table and sniff the saucers. They mustn't touch. When everyone has had a sniff, remove the tray and take off the blindfolds. The players must then write down what they think each saucer contained. A point is given for each correct guess.

Who's This?

Daniel Boorstin said it first, in his landmark book, *The Image*: 'The celebrity is a person who is known for his well-knownness.'

For this game the host must collect – from newspapers, magazines and their own photo album – a mass of pictures of celebrities. He sticks the faces of these famous figures on to a large piece of card. Teams are then given five minutes to jot down the names to fit the faces. Try to include a mix that will keep people guessing, so pick people from as wide a range of professions and time periods as possible: Diego Maradona mingling with Stalin, Henry the Second holding court with Harry Houdini, Gwyneth Paltrow and Gwyneth Dunwoody, and so on and so forth . . .

If you ask us, any day is a good day to get family and friends together and indulge in a round of two of Charades. However, it must be said that at certain times of year games are essential. Seasonal holidays are a chance for the whole clan to gather and enjoy each other's company – oases from the usual stresses of work and family life – and playing a game is the best way to get everyone, regardless of age, to mix and mingle. Over the next few pages you will find our selection of seasonal games for New Year, Valentine's, Easter, Hallowe'en and Christmas. And we've thrown in an Olympian touch of midsummer madness for good measure.

NEW YEAR'S EVE

• • •

The Scottish call it Hogmanay, the Catholics Saint Sylvester's Day, in Iceland it's Old Year's Day and in Wales it's Calennig. Whatever you call it and wherever you live, the end of one year and the start of the next is a good time to gather family and friends together, to give thanks for the year gone by, to let bygones be bygones (if necessary), to look forward to the year ahead . . . and to have a bit of a drink, a dance and a sing-song. Here are some games to get you in the mood.

Circle Talking
(aka the Yearly Round-Up)

This is a fab getting-to-know-you game that's ideal for playing at your New Year's Eve bash.

Two concentric circles are formed with the men facing outwards and the women facing inwards. To the accompaniment of music – 'Let's Start the New Year Right' by Bing Crosby is a classic, 'New Year's Day' by U2 is on topic but a tad on the depressing side, or you could plump for Gyles' favourite, 'New Year's Eve' by Snoop Dogg – the circles dance round in opposite directions.

When the circle stops everyone must talk to the person immediately opposite them on a topic announced by the host: personal highlight of your year; favourite album, film, play of the year, most embarrassing moment of the year; best night out of the year (this one of course!) . . . you get the idea.

When the two minutes have passed the music strikes up again and the circles dance around once more. Once all the topics, to say nothing of the players, have been exhausted, it's time to take a break and top up on refreshments.

First Footer

In Scottish folklore, the 'first footer' is the first person to cross the threshold of the house in the New Year, bringing with them luck for the coming twelve months plus a delicious fruitcake known as a 'black bun', a piece of shortbread, a lump of coal and a wee dram of whisky.

Tradition dictates that the 'first footer' should be a dark and handsome male, but, in our First Footer racing game, it is simply the winner, whoever that may be.

To play the game, gather all your guests in the run up to midnight. When there is one minute left to go, the race begins. The object of the race is not to be the first person to cross the finishing line – the threshold – but to be the first person to cross the finishing line immediately *after* the first stroke of midnight.

Once the starting whistle has blown players can move as slowly as they like, *but they must never stop moving*. If they do stop, they are disqualified, as is any player who crosses the line before midnight has struck. Once the chant of '*Ten . . . nine . . . eight . . . seven . . .*' begins, the remaining players will inch their way towards the door before all rushing to be the first across the threshold at the stroke of midnight; at which point all thoughts of competition are forgotten and everybody links arms and joins in for a rousing chorus of 'Auld Lang Syne'.

Never Look Back

N ew Year, New You! Now is not the time for looking back, and that's what this racing game is all about: never looking back and keeping your faith in what lies ahead.

Players split into pairs. One of each pair lines up at one end of the room and the other opposite him at the other end. The players on the far shores have to turn around and face the wall. Then the race begins. The players have to walk backwards to their team-mate, who will be waiting at the other end of the room shouting encouragement and forewarning their fellow player of any obstacles that are in the way. The winner is the player who reaches their team-mate first. Anyone caught looking back over their shoulder will be *immediately* disqualified.

If you want to make the game a little trickier for your guests you can strew the living-room floor with extra obstacles – cushions, waste-paper baskets, and the like – but if your friends have had a drop or two of festive cheer, as ours normally have on New Year's Eve, it is probably wisest to keep things simple.

New Year's Resolutions

The host-cum-question-master prepares a list of ten well-known personalities (or a combination of celebrities and fellow guests) – Britney Spears, Pope Francis, President Obama, Sherlock Holmes, the host, J. K. Rowling, Bart Simpson, Elvis Presley, Cousin Johnny, Mickey Mouse and Aunty Sue – and the players have to write a New Year resolution for each of them. Resolutions can be humorous or sincere. After five minutes all the guests read out their proposed resolutions and the assembled group vote for the best of the bunch.

VALENTINE'S DAY

* * *

Oh, the games people play in the name of love . . . *Happily, the four in this section are more likely to leave you with a tickled funny bone than a broken heart.*

Nobody knows very much about the original Saint Valentine, except that he was probably a priest who lived in Rome and was martyred for sheltering Christians from the Romans. His feast day is 14 February and coming, as it does, right in the middle of the month, it coincides with the date when, according to an ancient myth, birds begin to choose their mates. It is this coincidence that has made Saint Valentine the patron saint of lovers and turned 14 February into the day when people send one another Valentine tokens.

When it comes to sending a Valentine token – and it doesn't matter if it's a home-made card or an expensive heart-shaped box of chocolates – there is one golden rule that must never be broken: the token must be sent anonymously. Nobody must know you sent it and you must certainly not sign it. The girl or boy who gets it can guess that it was you who sent it, but it is something you must never tell them.

Forbidden Love Story

Players take it in turn to tell a famous love story. The aim is to stick to the facts and to speak true, but not to be discovered . . . You are not allowed to name any names or places. So your story can't begin, 'In fair Verona . . .' Nor would you want it to, as the idea is to tell the story, sticking to the facts, but to get as far as you can before the audience guesses whose story you are telling. It could be the tale of Romeo and Juliet, or David and Elton, or Richard Burton and Elizabeth Taylor, or Abelard and Eloise, or Kermit and Miss Piggy, or Cinderella and Prince Charming, or your host and . . . well, perhaps not.

The story-telling is done against the clock and the player who can tell the longest love story before the secret identity of the lovers is discovered is the winner.

'I love my love . . .'

This is a popular game with young children, especially little girls. Quite simply, to play the game players take it in turn to declare their love and do so by completing this sentence:

'I love my love because he/she is . . .'

The declarations are made alphabetically and in turn. So player one could say,

'I love my love because he is adventurous.'

Player two could follow:

'I love my love because she is beautiful.'

Player three:

'I love my love because he is charming.'

Player four:

'I love my love because he is daring . . .'

or dashing, or delightful or dotty . . . and so on.

It is not usually a requirement that the adjectives should be flattering: instead of being adorable, beautiful and charming, your love might be awkward, bald and careless.

Any player unable to think of an adjective beginning with the next letter of the alphabet drops out of the game, and the next player starts again with the letter A. Repetitions are not allowed and the last player left in is the winner.

If this version of the game is not challenging enough for your players, you can play the longer variation which goes like this.

'I love my love with an A because he is *adventurous*; I hate my love with an A because he is *angry*; his name is *Albert*; he lives in *Aberdeen* where he keeps *apes* which he feeds with *apples*.

'I love my love with a B because he is *brave*; I hate my love with a B because he is *beastly*; his name is *Bertram*; he lives in *Brisbane* where he keeps *bees* which he feeds on *biscuits*.

People usually leave out Q, X and Z because they are too difficult, though they can be done. Here's how:

I love my love with a Q because she is *quiet*; I hate my love with a Q because she is *quarrelsome*; her name is *Queenie*; she lives in *Queensland* where she keeps *quails* which she feeds on *quince*.

I love my love with an X because she is a *Xanthian*; I hate my love with an X because she is *xenophobic*; her name is *Xantippe*; she lives in *Xeres* where she keeps *xiphias* which she feeds on *xylose*.

I love my love with a Z because he is *zestful;* I hate my love with a Z because he is *zany*; his name is *Zorba*; he lives in *Zanzibar* where he keeps a *zebra* which he feeds on *zinc*.

Feel free to adapt the game to suit the age, character and vocabulary range of those playing. You can make it as simple or as complicated as you like.

Gyles says: In case you wondering, a Xanthian is someone who comes from the town of Xanthius, an ancient town in Asia Minor; someone who is xenophobic can't stand foreigners; Xantippe was the name of the wife of Socrates; Xeres is the name of an Andalusian town famous for its wine; a xiphia is a kind of swordfish and xylose is an unusual form of sugar. Oh yes, further proof that my time in *Countdown*'s Dictionary Corner has been far from wasted.

Postman's Knock

This is an innocent and ancient pastime, which probably pre-dates the first reported postman in 1529.

One of the male players leaves the room and paces up and down the corridor anxiously. The other players, meanwhile, give themselves numbers – even numbers for the men, uneven for the women. When every player has a number, they all call out 'We're ready!' and the outsider knocks firmly on the door three times.

'Who's there?' cry the players in the room.

''Tis the postman,' replies the outsider, 'and I have something here for number 3' (or 7 or 11 or any other uneven number). 'Come and get it!'

So number 3 has to go out and join the postman, who gives her a kiss.

The pair then return to the main room and another player – female this time – leaves the room and becomes the postmistress. The remaining players choose new numbers and, after she has knocked, the postmistress declares that she has something for number 4 (or any other even number) and out the lucky fellow goes to claim his Valentine smacker.

Soulmates

S oulmates is the perfect getting-to-know-you game to play at your Valentine's Day singles bash. Play it properly and there won't be any lonely hearts by the end of the evening.

As each guest arrives, the host whispers the name of a notorious lover into their ear and they have to set about finding their partner, not by crudely calling out 'I'm Antony, where's Cleopatra?', but by going round the other guests and talking to them individually. So, for example, if you were to ask the lovely lady standing over by the fireplace where she was born, and she were to reply 'Alexandria, Egypt', you'd be in luck.

If obvious lovers are chosen – Wills and Kate, Adam and Eve, Simon Cowell and himself (only joking, Si) – the company will have paired off before the first cocktail. However, if care is taken in selecting the soulmates (for example, Victoria and Albert, Tristan and Isolde, Fish and Chips), the game will be a good deal more rewarding.

Gyles says: If, by any chance, there are more women than men, one of the male guests can take on the role of Henry VIII, Warren Beatty or Silvio Berlusconi. Should there be a plethora of men, one of the women can always be Elizabeth Taylor, Zsa Zsa Gabor or Beverly Nina Avery. Miss Avery, a barmaid from Los Angeles, has had fourteen husbands and is said to be the world's most married woman.

Writing Romance

This isn't a competitive game, merely a chance to channel the group's inner Barbara Cartland or Marian Keyes . . .

Select a passage from a romantic novel – a page from your favourite Mills & Boon is ideal. Alternatively, you can make up your own story. Write it down or copy the passage from the book, *but* leave a blank where all the adjectives should be.

Gather your guests together and get each of them in turn to give you a random adjective. You must put whatever they say in the blank spaces in the order the adjectives are given to you. The guests will have no idea of the story of course, and may propose some wildly inappropriate adjectives; let's certainly hope so! When all the blanks are filled in, read the story out to the assembled crowd. The results are often hilarious, if not wildly romantic.

EASTER

• • •

For Christians, just as Good Friday is the saddest day of the year, Easter Day is the happiest; it is happier even than Christmas Day itself. The churches are given a thorough clean, the brasses are polished, fresh candles are lit, spring flowers are displayed everywhere. It used to be traditional to wear new clothes on Easter Day and our Bonnet Race is the perfect opportunity to revive the tradition.

So, here to add along a competitive twist to your Easter celebrations, are the Brandreths' Easter games favourites.

Bonnet Race

This game is always fun but can be even more so if players have made their own Easter bonnets. This can be done quite simply with some cardboard, glue, ribbons and sparkly bits . . . but that's for another book. Here, all we can tell you is that to play Bonnet Race you will need either a bonnet for each player or, if that is not possible, one bonnet per team. The most important thing is that the bonnets (or hats) must have ribbons that can be tied underneath the chin, in the style of traditional Easter bonnets.

Players divide into teams and stand in rows. If every player has his or her own bonnet, this is what happens. All the players hold their bonnets in their hands. On the command 'Go!' the leader of each team dons his bonnet and ties the ribbon in a bow under his chin. He then turns and curtsies to the second player in line. The curtsy is the cue for the second player to don her bonnet and tie her ribbon. When she has done so, she turns and curtsies to the third player, and so it goes on down the line. The first team to have everyone in the line wearing their done-up bonnets properly wins the race.

If there are only as many bonnets as there are teams, this is what happens. On the command 'Go!' the leader of each team dons his bonnet and ties the bonnet's ribbon into a bow beneath his chin. He then turns to the second player in his team and she undoes the bow, takes the bonnet, puts it on, ties the bow and turns to the third player, and so it goes on down the line. The first team to cover every head and get the bonnet neatly tied on to the last head wins.

Easter Egg Wobble

This game is not as is easy as it sounds. An Easter egg is placed on a table at one side of the room. All you have to do is go and eat it, but, and it is a bit of a big BUT, first you must place your forehead on the handle of an Easter parasol, place the point on the ground, and turn round six times with your eyes fixed on the ground as you do so. Then off you go!

Saethryd says: If you don't happen to have a parasol hanging around, a bog-standard brolly will do just as well; and a broom handle or big stick might even cut it if you are desperate. This game can be played one by one or, if you have enough umbrellas or parasols or big sticks, it can be played as a race.

Rory says: I love this game!

Hopping Bunnies

The object of the game is to hop the farthest while making progressively longer hops, till only one player is left victorious and the others are hopping mad.

Lay two lengths of string parallel along the floor, approximately a foot (that's 30 cm in metric) apart. Now angle them so that they are a foot apart at one end but get gradually further and further apart till there is about five or six feet (a metre and a half plus) of distance between them at the far end.

Contestants line up and take it in turns to hop back and forth across the two lines of string, hopping a wider distance with each hop as they travel down the course.

The player who gets the farthest before failing to hop across both lines in a single leap is the winner.

Indoor Egg and Spoon Race

Like the Bonnet Race (page 435), the fun of the Indoor Egg and Spoon Race can be doubled if you get contestants to prep their own eggs beforehand. Provide as many hard-boiled eggs as there are contestants and lay out paints, brushes, glitter and all other manner of decorative delights on the kitchen table so that racers can personalise their eggs before the grand event begins.

Once all the eggs are dry and Easter lunch has been eaten (and properly digested), players collect their eggs, and a spoon, and all line up at the end of the course. The whistle blows, and they're off. Balancing egg on spoon the players rush to be the first to cross the finishing line.

If their egg falls from their spoon, they have to pick it up and go back to the start. The first to make it all the way to the finish is rewarded with another egg – a chocolate one.

Variation

The players are divided into two teams, forming parallel lines. Each player is given a spoon which he holds in his mouth, and an egg is placed in the spoon of the first player in each team. The first player has to transfer the egg from their spoon to the spoon of the second player, and so on down the line. No player may use their hands to touch the egg. If it falls to the floor then the player who dropped it must go down on hands and knees and scoop up the egg with the spoon still held in their mouth. The first team to successfully transfer the egg to the player at the end of the line wins.

Paper Bag Pinata

The origins of the piñata are much debated. Although these colourful papier mâché cases filled with sweets are now most associated with Mexico, they are thought to have originated in China. The Spanish adopted them at some point around the Middle Ages as part of their Easter celebrations, signalling the end of Lent.

Nowadays they are used at fiestas all over the world for any occasion, but this homemade version brings the piñata back to basics, as well as its roots, and is ideal for an Easter party. The kids will love it.

To construct your no-fuss homemade piñata, simply place a selection of sweets and chocolate in a large paper bag with handles. (If you put two bags inside each other the game will last longer). If you want to you can decorate the bag beforehand with tassles, ribbons, glitter and whatever Easter paraphernalia you have left over from making your bonnets.

Hang the bag from a length of string and then attach it, either to a doorway (you can hang it from a little nail above the doorframe without making much of a mark) or a washing-line if it is a sunny enough day to play outside. Get all the children, and adults if they fancy a go, to line up and then pass the first participant a big stick. Each player gets one minute to bash the bag as hard as they like. If they break the bag and the sweets come tumbling down, lucky them. If not, it's on to the next in line.

If you want to make the game a little harder, you can blindfold partici-pants before it is their turn to bash the piñata. If you do this, make sure that everyone is a safe distance away as you want to make sure it's just the piñata that is getting a bashing.

Pin the Tail on the Easter Bunny

Pin the Tail on the Easter Bunny is a twist on the children's party classic Pin the Tail on the Donkey. In preparation, get the artist in your family to draw a big picture of a bunny – sideways on – on a piece of paper at least A3 or bigger.

Fix your picture of the Easter Bunny on to a wall. Then gather your Easter chicks around you and blindfold the first one before handing her a bunny 'tail' – a cotton-wool ball with one side dipped in a craft glue (something like Copydex, for example). Turn the blindfolded player around three times and then send her off in the right direction to pin her tail on the bunny.

Write each player's name next to their tail. The player who gets their tail closest to the correct spot is the winner.

Rory says: What do you get if you pour a cup of tea down a rabbit hole? A hot cross bunny!

MIDSUMMER MADNESS

• • •

In the summertime, when the weather
is fine, we tend to be out and about enjoying
the sunshine, but just in case you find yourself
at a loss one July afternoon, we suggest
you while away some happy hours with a
games extravaganza (medals optional) . . .

Garden Olympics

If you've got plenty of friends round one afternoon in the summer holidays and you are looking for something to do, why not embrace the spirit of London 2012 and put on your own Garden Olympics? It's also a good way of keeping warm on those less-than-balmy English summer days.

You will need plenty of garden (or a large-enough living room if the weather's not co-operating) to run along, a starting line, a finishing post, and an umpire who can organise each race and see there's no cheating.

Here are some ideas for different races you can stage as part of your Garden Olympics.

1. A hopping race, first using right feet only, then using left feet only.
2. A head-over-heels race, with the players somersaulting down the course.
3. A three-legged race, with the players in pairs.
4. A water race, with the players carrying buckets of water and being disqualified if they spill any. (Not necessarily one for the living room.)
5. A hop-skip-and-jump race in which players have to hop, skip and jump their way along the course.
6. A piggy-back race, with the players forming pairs and one riding on the back of the other.

7. A wheelbarrow race, with the players again forming pairs and one player acting as the wheelbarrow, while the other player pushes them from behind and holds their legs.

8. A ball-throwing race, with the players in pairs having to throw a ball from one to another as they race along the track. If a player drops a ball she and her partner are disqualified.

9. A backwards race, with all the players running backwards.

10. A four-legged race. You play this in exactly the same way as a three-legged race, except, of course, that you have four legs because three players, not two, are strapped together.

HALLOWE'EN

• • •

All Hallows Eve takes place on 31
October, the day before All Saints Day in
the Christian calendar. As night falls the
boundaries between the living and dead are
blurred and the spirits of the deceased rise
again to cause mischief and mayhem. The
day has strong pagan roots which pre-date
the Christian festival and, in modern times,
the American tradition of trick-or-treating,
and the international horror film industry
have added extra elements to the celebration.
At Brandreth Towers we embrace progress
(as well as any excuse to dress up) and
are completely on board with trick-
or-treating, as well as apple-bobbing,
pumpkin carving and fiendish frolics
of all kinds. Enjoy our selection of
Hallowe'en games, both old and new.

Apple Ducking

This game is *the* traditional Hallowe'en favourite. It goes back hundreds of years and no doubt has connections to the end of the harvest and the Gaelic festival of Samhain, which marks the moment that autumn turns to winter.

Fill a large bowl with water and in it float half a dozen apples. Place the bowl on the floor and, if you are indoors, surround it with towels or newspaper in case of splashes. To play the game, each player must kneel by the bowl, their hands behind their back, and extract an apple from the water using only their mouth and teeth.

The more sedate version of the game involves one player ducking at a time with, say, a two-minute time limit for the ducking. The more rumbustious version takes the form of a race, with several or all of the players ducking for apples at the same time, the first player to lift an apple from the water being the winner. When playing this version, the fun (which may involve bumped heads and spilled water) can be enhanced by using apples which have been coated liberally with honey or syrup.

Saethryd says: For those of you who love a good detective story and a spooky seasonal read, I thoroughly recommend Agatha Christie's 1969 novel, *Hallowe'en Party*, in which Poirot has to solve the mystery of a girl found murdered in an apple-ducking tub.

Execution

Execution is a small, sinister game that has somehow survived the abolition of the death penalty . . . *mwah-ha-ha-ha!*

> *Rory says*: What was that?!?
> *Saethryd says*: It was meant to be an evil cackle, dude.
> *Rory says*: Seriously? You are *so* embarrassing . . .

The players sit in a circle with the tips of their raised forefingers meeting in the centre. The executioner, who stands outside the circle and should at least be wearing a black pillowcase over his head, slips a running noose round the fingers and holds the end of the string. He cries 'Death!' and jerks up the string. The players whip their fingers away and anyone whose finger is caught in the noose is sent off to the knacker's yard . . . or to make coffee, depending how seriously you take the game.

Ghosts

Young children love this game and it can provide a bit of a giggle, and a welcome relief, from some of the spookier aspects of the night.

Divide the players into two teams and get one team to leave the room. The members of the team that leaves the room now cover themselves with large white sheets. Now dressed as ghosts, they then return to the room, making suitably spooky sounds as they come, and do their best to frighten their opponents. While the opponents are being scared out of their wits, they must attempt to identify the ghosts. They cannot touch them and they cannot question them, but they can ask them to make ghostly noises and to perform minor tasks and tests of supernatural skill. Once a ghost has been revealed, he takes off his sheet and sits down.

When all the spooks have been uncovered, the teams change places for the second round.

The Horror Game

This is not so much a jolly game as a ghastly experience; but it's unmissable, for all that.

The host gathers his guests around a table and in complete darkness tells them the story of the murder that was committed in that very room . . . indeed, as it happens, on the very spot where they are all now sitting. The host describes the murder in a way which would have warmed the heart of Dr Crippen (had he had one) and should chill his audience to the marrow. He goes on to tell of how the murderer, having killed his victim, dismembered the body in order to hide it. As each part of the corpse is mentioned, the host actually passes it round the table.

How? Not necessarily by carving up his mother-in-law for the occasion. More usually, by passing simulated limbs to his guests. The victim's head can be a cabbage or an overripe melon. His eyes can be soft grapes. His brains, a damp sponge. His tongue, a slice of Spam. His toes, baby carrots (the tinned variety are the most effective).

When the host has concluded his grim tale, he turns on the lights picks up those guests that have fainted and announces that he never wishes to see any of them ever again.

And he won't. If you want to lose friends – and many people do – this is the game for you. And if you have an immensely ancient and wealthy aunt who stubbornly refuses to meet her maker, this is the game for her.

Musical Torch

This game can be quite spooky and goes down very well at Hallowe'en parties and with children who love to frighten one another.

The players sit on the floor in a circle and all the lights are turned out. One player is given a lighted torch and when the music plays the torch is passed from hand to hand around the group. Whoever is holding the torch when the music stops drops out. The last player left in is the winner.

To make the game as eerie as possible, hold the torch just below your chin and while the music is playing make all sorts of ghostly noises.

Witch Hunt

This is a spooky game that can be lots of fun at a Hallowe'en party, provided none of the players is easily frightened. A witch is chosen and sent to hide somewhere in the house. As soon as the witch has had time to hide, *all* the lights are turned out and the witch-hunters set out to find the witch. If the hunters call out 'Where are you, witch?', the witch, who can move about as much as she likes (or dares) in the dark, has to answer with a witch-like cackle.

Whoever catches the witch becomes the witch for the next round.

CHRISTMAS

• • •

*It's the most wonderful time of
the year. Need more be said?*

A Baby is Born

This is a fun game to play at a Christmas gathering, either on the day or in the run-up. When you invite your guests over, ask them each to bring a picture of themselves as a baby. When they arrive take the picture from them and either pin it up on a board, place it on a table or whack it on the fridge with a magnet, depending on what kind of soirée it is.

When all the guests, and pictures, are in place, everyone has to write down which baby they think is which guest. The winner is the guest with the most correct guesses, and they get an extra glass of eggnog.

Cinders' Slipper

This is a great ice-breaker that's perfect to play if you are having a Christmas party for friends, family, neighbours and colleagues, some of whom might not know each other. It takes its inspiration from one of our family's favourite Christmas traditions: pantomime.

As the guests arrive they are greeted by the host and hostess who are on their knees at the front door. They are on their knees in order to have quick and easy access to the feet of their friends. Every time a lady steps through the door, the host removes her left shoe. Every time a gentleman comes in, the hostess takes off his right shoe.

As soon as everyone has arrived the host and hostess dump their collection of shoes in the middle of the room and invite everybody to pick up one shoe (not their own) and find a partner whose foot it will fit.

The game is a back-to-front race and the last person remaining with a foot unshod is the winner. The prize: a sip of champagne (or red plonk) from the shoe of the victor's choice. (Considerate hosts will warn their guests so they can come equipped with fresh socks, un-holey tights and a spare pair of galoshes.)

Gyles says: This game takes its inspiration from the story of Cinderella, who lost one of her slippers at Prince Charming's ball. The pantomime of *Cinderella* looms large in the Brandreth family mythology, not only because I have played Baron Hardup in panto a couple times, but more so because it was at an audition for a student production of *Cinderella* that I met Saethryd's mother . . .

Merry Christmas
and Happy New Year

This game is a festive Buzz-Fizz (see above, page 57). It can be rather tricky to master when buzzing after too much festive fizz, but it can be enjoyed by players of every age, so long as they can count!

What's involved is this. The players take it in turn to count from one to infinity, with each player saying a different number – but the numbers 5 and 7, and multiples of 5 and 7, must *never* be mentioned. Instead, when you get to a 5 or a multiple of 5 you say 'Merry Christmas', and when you get to a 7 or a multiple of 7 you say 'Happy New Year'. When you reach a multiple of 5 *and* 7 (35, for example) you say 'Merry Christmas and Happy New Year'. To get you going, here's how it goes from numbers 1 to 21:

1

2

3

4

Merry Christmas

6

Happy New Year

8

9

Merry Christmas

11

12

13

Happy New Year

Merry Christmas

16

Happy New Year

18

19

Merry Christmas

Happy New Year

Anyone caught saying one of the forbidden numbers or coming out with 'Happy New Year' instead of 'Merry Christmas', or vice versa, drops out. The last player left counting is the winner. When played at great speed, this is a very exciting and entertaining game.

Mince Pie Munch

Players divide into two teams, with an equal number of players in each team. Each team has to sit in a row, and each player has a mince pie and a glass of sherry (or milk or juice for the younger players) in front of them.

When the signal is given, the first player has to turn round and feed their mince pie to the player behind them. The player being fed has to keep their hands behind their back the whole time. Once the mince pie has been munched, the first player has to get the second player to drink their drink; again the second player must keep their hands behind their back.

Once their pie has been eaten and their drink has been drunk, it is the second player's turn to about face and start feeding and watering the player behind. When the end of the row is reached, the last player runs to the front and feeds the first player their mince pie and sherry.

The first team to finish the festive fare is announced the winner and the players get to wear paper hats for the rest of the day.

Santa Packed my Stocking

This is a quiet word game that goes down very well with a third helping of Christmas cake and a tenth mince pie. The players take it in turn to say what Santa Claus, Father Christmas, Old Saint Nick, or whatever it is you like to call him, put in their stockings, and as the game progresses each player has to remember an ever-lengthening list of Christmas trifles.

For example, player number one might begin, 'Santa packed my stocking and in it he put a tangerine.'

Player number two would then have to repeat what the first player had said and add their own item. They might say: 'Santa packed my stocking and in it he put a tangerine and a copy of *A Christmas Carol*.'

Player number three now adds their item: 'Santa packed my stocking and in it he put a tangerine, a copy of *A Christmas Carol* and a yo-yo.'

And so the game continues to go round and round the group, with every player repeating everything that has gone before and adding a fresh item of their own whenever it's their turn. Anyone who forgets an item or who gets an item in the wrong order drops out, and when there is only one player left in, that player has won.

It is good to end with a quiet game, isn't it?

INDEX